English Names
of Wild Flowers

English Names
of Wild Flowers

*A List Recommended by the Botanical
Society of the British Isles*

JOHN G. DONY
Past President of the Botanical Society of the British Isles

FRANKLYN PERRING
*Biological Records Centre, Monks Wood Experimental
Station*

CATHERINE M. ROB
Past President of the Yorkshire Naturalists' Union

BUTTERWORTHS
for
THE BOTANICAL SOCIETY OF THE BRITISH ISLES

THE BUTTERWORTH GROUP

ENGLAND
Butterworth & Co (Publishers) Ltd
London: 88 Kingsway, WC2B 6AB

AUSTRALIA
Butterworths Pty Ltd
Sydney: 586 Pacific Highway, NSW 2067
Melbourne: 343 Little Collins Street, 3000
Brisbane: 240 Queen Street, 4000

CANADA
Butterworth & Co (Canada) Ltd
Toronto: 14 Curity Avenue, 374

NEW ZEALAND
Butterworths of New Zealand Ltd
Wellington: 26-28 Waring Taylor Street, 1

SOUTH AFRICA
Butterworth & Co (South Africa) (Pty) Ltd
Durban: 152-154 Gale Street

First published in 1974

ISBN 0 408 70563 9 standard
     0 408 70564 7 limp

Typeset by Amos Typesetters, Hockley, Essex
Printed in England by Butler & Tanner Ltd, Frome and London

Foreword

Dr. S. M. Walters
*Director, University Botanic Garden, Cambridge
and President, B.S.B.I.*

As a young and impressionable student in Cambridge, I received my warning against the use of vernacular names for plants from Humphrey Gilbert-Carter, the first Director of the Botanic Garden. This admonition was so happily worded that I could never forget it . . . 'There are only *four* English names', Humphrey would boom, 'Baby's Breath' (white-flowered plants), 'Old Men's Britches' (anything coloured), 'Knobbly-Stalks' (any sort of grass, sedge or rush) and 'Kecks' (Umbellifers). But Humphrey's apparent contempt for the vernacular names was really only an inoculation technique; his extraordinary interest in languages, living and dead, ensured that *all* names of plants interested him (especially those from Eastern languages), and his overriding concern was that his students should learn to use the scientific, Latin names because that was the internationally-accepted language of Botany.

Of course there is a place for Latin names, and a place for vernacular names, and I am delighted that the Society has approached the problem presented by the bewildering variety of the latter so sensibly. The search for the *via media* increasingly seems to me to be the 'English way', and this excellent, practical publication represents this important tradition at its best. By all means let us have a 'standard' book of English names for reference; but let us not forget two things. Firstly, it is parochial and for internal use; the Latin name remains the scientific, international one. Secondly, no-one is trying to dictate what anyone else should call his or her familiar wild flower. It would be a colourless world if all the regional variants in speech and dialect disappeared, and long may the 'Paigles' flourish with the 'Cowslips'!

A List of Recommended English Names for British Wild Plants

INTRODUCTION

The need to apply English names to wild plants is comparatively recent. Our ancestors were content originally to give such names only to plants for which they had a use with the result that the English names of many of our trees date back to the Anglo-Saxon period. This may be seen in a number of place names: Aspley (Asplea 969) was an aspen-tree clearing, Salford (Saleford 1086) was a ford by sallows, etc. In the same manner plants which were edible received names which could vary from place to place. Whortleberry, bilberry, huckleberry, whorts and blaeberry were all applied to one species. Gorse and furze appear early but could have had reference also to juniper or any other quick-growing small bushes used for fuel. Although medieval documents contain abundant references to wild plants some doubt often remains as to their precise identity.

Some persistent weeds also received names which were local in their use. The various names applied to *Aegopodium podagraria*—Bishop's-weed, Pope's-weed, goutweed, Herb Gerard, ground-elder—illustrates the many appellations of a plant with which so many people have had direct contact.

The introduction of printing brought a measure of consistency with the use of English names for many wild plants by the herbalists. These found some names already widely used but they were more often forced to invent names by translating those in Greek or Latin.

The early botanical works were in Latin usually giving long names for plants which were in the nature of descriptions rather than simple names. The introduction of binomials by Linnaeus in his *Species Plantarum* (1753) brought not only stability to nomenclature but a remarkable increase in the study of plants. In the later years of the eighteenth century came the publication of the first Floras in English bringing with them an increased need

1

for English names of the plants to take their place side by side with the simplified Latin names. By this time most wild plants had English names, many too coarse and vulgar for use by young ladies who were being urged to take up the study of plants. Any names which were suitable and generally accepted were used but as had been the case with the herbalists the newer school of botanists had to resort to invention. This they often proceeded to do with a literal translation of the new Latin name into English. The English name frequently became a simple means of remembering the Latin name and vice versa. A plant with the specific name *latifolia* would carry the adjective 'broad-leaved' to its English name even if a closely allied species had leaves just as broad or even broader. It was, however, a good system and by the time of Bentham and Hooker's superb *Flora* (1887) it could well have appeared that a stable position had been reached in which each wild plant had its Latin name with a corresponding English name both of which would last for all time.

Time has undermined the stability of the Latin names as taxonomists have found that many names have been wrongly applied—what we had known for so long as *Scrophularia aquatica* must now be *S. auriculata,* to quote just one of many instances. The study of botany is not static and research has shown that many a large genus of plants could be better considered to consist of a number of smaller genera. Some smaller genera have been shown to comprise one large genus. In many instances these changes may be a matter of opinion but it is very necessary for the study of botany in the British Isles to be consistent with what is accepted elsewhere. In recent years what we may have known as dogwood or cornel or dogberry or dogberry-tree has had almost as many Latin names in *Cornus sanguinea, Thelycrania sanguinea* and *Swida sanguinea.*

Authors of modern floras have not adhered strictly to the English names of the Bentham and Hooker period, having often had good reasons for their individual departures. There is now a situation which is confusing enough to botanists but even more so to an increasing number, particularly those concerned with nature conservation, who claim no botanical knowledge but need to apply an English name to a particular plant with some confidence so that others will know to which species of plant they refer. It became clear that the only way of making progress towards stability of English names would be the production of a list of recommended names for wild plants. It was with this in view that we were appointed in 1968 as a Working Party by the Council of the Botanical Society of the British Isles to prepare such a list.

We found that our task had been faced before by J. F. Rayner whose *Standard catalogue of English names of our wild flowers* (1926) while in many respects excellent had been little used. In the first instance we listed all the English names for each wild plant which were used in the fourteen works which we considered to be in most general use. In the majority of cases there was no doubt at all as to the name which would be the most acceptable. In the remaining doubtful cases we were influenced by the names used by Rayner and those used in Clapham, Tutin and Warburg's *Flora of the British Isles,* second edition (1962) and McClintock and Fitter's *Pocket Guide to Wild Flowers* (1956). The *Pocket Guide* we considered of great importance as a widely used flora giving priority to English names.

As a result of our preliminary investigation a list was prepared which was circulated to the members of the Council of the Botanical Society of the British Isles and to many others who had expressed an interest. We received numerous suggestions and helpful criticisms, each of which we carefully considered, being grateful to all who made them but especially so to Mr. J. E. Lousley, whose advice was always sound, Mr. D. McClintock, who for obvious reasons had given great thought to our problem, and Mr. R. Chancellor, of the Weed Research Organisation, who wisely insisted that the English names of weeds should be those known to farmers. Our final list produced here is based on principles which may demand some explanation.

One English name only for a species is adopted. We considered carefully a number of instances in which two English names were used widely, e.g. ling and heather for *Calluna vulgaris.* Such apparently good cases were numerous. We decided finally that alternative names would cause confusion and contradict the requirement that the Working Party recommend a separate name for each wild plant.

Inappropriate names are rejected. These are usually literal translations of Latin names which are not appropriate. We have preferred Broad-leaved Willowherb to Mountain Willowherb for *Epilobium montanum* as this is not in Britain an exclusively mountain species.

A binomial system is adopted. Some English names, e.g. holly, may stand in their own right but in those cases where a number of closely allied species bear the same English generic name, e.g. vetch, binomials are strictly adhered to. We have converted trinomials, which were often ambiguous, into binomials by using hyphens, and created 'English' sub-genera. The reader will find male-ferns, water-speedwells, etc. which we hope will eliminate such ambiguities as scaly male fern and blue water speedwell. In following this principle we are fully aware that ambiguities still remain with small-white orchid and early-purple orchid but we have resisted the temptation to make sub-genera of white-orchids and purple-orchids having in them only one species.

English generic names are limited to one family of plants. An application of this principle may be seen with the cabbages which we have limited to the Cruciferae. St. Patrick's-cabbage is not a true cabbage as it belongs to the Saxifragaceae and it is in consequence hyphenated. We have made three exceptions to this rule.

1. Horse-radish although with the other radishes in the Cruciferae we consider far enough removed from them to stand in its own right.

2. White bryony and black bryony each stand alone as it is not clear whether the true bryony is *Bryonia* (Cucurbitaceae) or *Tamus* (Dioscoreaceae).

3. Greater celandine and lesser celandine each stand alone as it is not clear whether the true celandine is *Chelidonium* (Papaveraceae) or *Ranunculus ficaria* (Ranunculaceae).

We have considered the true chestnut to be *Castanea* (Fagaceae) and the true purslane to be *Portulaca* (Portulacaceae).

Plant names from other families forming part of a longer name are hyphenated. This follows the sub-generic principle and is seen most clearly amongst the 'water' plants, e.g. water-dropwort, water-lily, water-violet. We have adopted water-cress to show that this belongs to the bigger group of cresses although watercress is now in common usage.

In following this principle we have made a major exception for the grasses. We have applied 'rush' in its restricted sense to *Juncus* and 'sedge' to *Carex* but find no genus to which 'grass' can be so restricted. We have, however, restricted 'grass' when used with a hyphen to the true grasses (Gramineae). We have made cottongrass one word as the cottongrasses are not true grasses and grass is used here as a general term. We experienced some difficulty with blue-eyed-grass and yellow-eyed-grass which might have been solved by making a genus of eyed-grasses and by so doing making an exception to a principle which had worked well.

Otherwise multi-syllable words are unhyphenated unless a hyphen is needed to make the meaning clear. Thus we have hornbeam, whitebeam, longleaf and oysterplant, but thorow-wax and yellow-wort.

THE LIST

This is in two parts. We gave serious consideration to having one list only in systematic order with a comprehensive index but rejected this in favour of two lists in alphabetic order in the hope that this would be more useful to other than botanists.

The Latin name to English name list

This includes all Latin names, other than synonyms, used in:

The Concise British Flora in Colour by W. Keble Martin (1965).

The Pocket Guide to Wild Flowers by D. McClintock and R. S. R. Fitter (1956).

Flora of the British Isles, second edition, by A. R. Clapham, T. G. Tutin and E. F. Warburg (1962).

Excursion Flora of the British Isles, second edition, by A. R. Clapham, T. G. Tutin and E. F. Warburg (1968).

List of British Vascular Plants by J. E. Dandy (1958).

Nomenclatural changes in the 'List of British Vascular Plants' by J. E. Dandy, *Watsonia,* **7,** 159–178 (1969).

Priority is given in the reverse order to which the above are listed. The Latin name which appears with a corresponding English name is that which British botanists generally consider now (1973) to be the most acceptable name.

The English name to Latin name list

This gives cross references to sub-generic English names and to other closely connected English names. Authors are not given for the Latin names as we are of the opinion that most of those who use the list will not need them. Any who may wish to use them should refer to the works listed above, one at least of which we think we may safely assume every reader will have access to. Authors are, however, given in the second list only, for names subject to the few nomenclatural changes recommended by Dandy in 1969 in a work to which fewer readers will have access.

Limitations of the list

We have not attempted to find names for microspecies, for all subspecies and for a number of rare species so closely allied to other species that few botanists can distinguish them. Our failure to do so affects mainly the microspecies of *Rubus* (brambles), *Hieracium* (hawkweeds) *Taraxacum* (dandelions), and *Euphrasia* (eyebrights), some closely allied roses (*Rosa*) and some species pairs. We strongly recommend that when an expert determination has been made the correct Latin name, preferably with the author quoted, be used with the English name.

The plants listed are mainly native species and colonists but a few of the frequent alien species are included. We considered carefully the inclusion of more aliens but were soon aware that the alien flora of Britain much exceeds the rest. The difficulty of deciding which additional aliens to include was no less than that of finding an appropriate name for them.

The use of capital letters

These should be used always for the Latin generic names. For the English names we recommend that they be used as they are printed in the list for labels, captions to illustrations, notes on individual plants and lists of plants arranged in columns. In the text of articles, nature trail guides and lists of plants in running order we recommend that, with obvious exceptions, the capital letter should be dispensed with. We regret that we have not been able to give an indication of what these exceptions should be. It would be better to write: 'This is an oak-hornbeam wood with hazel coppice, a ground vegetation consisting of dog's mercury, hairy St. Johns'-wort and wood anemone and with wide rides supporting two unusual brambles (*Rubus erraticus* Sudre and *R.griffithianus* Rogers),' rather than 'This is an Oak-Hornbeam wood with Hazel coppice, a ground vegetation consisting of Dog's Mercury, Hairy St. John's-wort and Wood Anemone and with wide rides supporting two unusual Brambles (*Rubus erraticus* Sudre and *R.griffithianus* Rogers).'

The use of the list

We hope that some priority may be given to the names recommended here by authors generally, but especially those of local floras, of articles intended for the general reader, of nature trail guides and of reports on sites such as nature reserves. At the same time we hope that regional and local names will long continue to be used but in a secondary and supplementary manner. We would much regret their passing and for this reason mainly prefer what is presented here to be a recommended rather than a standard list.

Not every wild plant name in this list is acceptable to each one of us or, in some cases, to the three of us collectively. As a working party we have given way individually to the pressure of each other's arguments and to the force of opinion of others whose judgment seemed more sound than our own. We hope that the list will be received in this spirit and that its use will help to establish some stability in place of the present situation which is in so many respects confusing.

Latin–English

Acaena anserinifolia	Pirri-pirri-bur
Acanthus mollis	Bear's-breech
Acer campestre	Field Maple
platanoides	Norway M.
pseudoplatanus	Sycamore
Aceras anthropophorum	Man Orchid
Achillea millefolium	Yarrow
ptarmica	Sneezewort
Acinos arvensis	Basil Thyme
Aconitum anglicum *see*	
A.napellus	
napellus	Monk's-hood
Acorus calamus	Sweet-flag
Actaea spicata	Baneberry
Adiantum capillus-veneris	Maidenhair Fern
Adonis annua	Pheasant's-eye
Adoxa moschatellina	Moschatel
Aegopodium podagraria	Ground-elder
Aesculus hippocastanum	Horse-chestnut
Aethusa cynapium	Fool's Parsley
Agrimonia eupatoria	Agrimony
odorata *see* A.procera	
procera	Fragrant A.

Agropyron caninum	Bearded Couch
donianum	Don's C.
junceiforme	Sand C.
pungens	Sea C.
repens	Common C.
Agrostemma githago	Corncockle
Agrostis canina	Brown Bent
gigantea	Black B.
semiverticillata	Water B.
setacea	Bristle B.
stolonifera	Creeping B.
tenuis	Common B.
Aira caryophyllea	Silver Hair-grass
praecox	Early H.
Ajuga chamaepitys	Ground-pine
pyramidalis	Pyramidal Bugle
reptans	Bugle
Alchemilla alpina	Alpine Lady's-mantle
vulgaris	Lady's-mantle
Alisma gramineum	Ribbon-leaved Water-plantain
lanceolatum	Narrow-leaved W.
plantago-aquatica	Water-plantain
Alliaria petiolata	Garlic Mustard
Allium ampeloprasum	Wild Leek
babingtonii	Babington's L.
carinatum	Keeled Garlic
oleraceum	Field G.
paradoxum	Few-flowered Leek
schoenoprasum	Chives
scorodoprasum	Sand Leek
sphaerocephalon	Round-headed L.
triquetrum	Three-cornered L.
ursinum	Ramsons
vineale	Wild Onion
Alnus glutinosa	Alder
incana	Grey A.
Alopecurus aequalis	Orange Foxtail
alpinus	Alpine F.

Alopecurus—*continued*
   bulbosus   Bulbous Foxtail
   geniculatus   Marsh F.
   myosuroides   Black-grass
   pratensis   Meadow Foxtail

Althaea hirsuta   Rough Marsh-mallow
   officinalis   Marsh-mallow

Alyssum alyssoides   Small Alison

Amaranthus hybridus   Green Amaranth
   retroflexus   Common A.

Ambrosia artemisiifolia   Ragweed

Amelanchier confusa   Juneberry

Ammi majus   Bullwort

Ammophila arenaria   Marram

Anacamptis pyramidalis   Pyramidal Orchid

Anagallis arvensis   Scarlet Pimpernel
   arvensis subsp.foemina *see*
      A.foemina
   foemina   Blue P.
   minima   Chaffweed
   tenella   Bog Pimpernel

Anaphalis margaritacea   Pearly Everlasting

Anchusa arvensis *see*
      Lycopsis arvensis
   officinalis   Alkanet

Andromeda polifolia   Bog Rosemary

Anemone apennina   Blue Anemone
   nemorosa   Wood A.
   pulsatilla *see* Pulsatilla
      vulgaris
   ranunculoides   Yellow A.

Angelica archangelica   Garden Angelica
   sylvestris   Wild A.

Anisantha *see* Bromus

Anogramma leptophylla	Jersey Fern
Antennaria dioica	Mountain Everlasting
Anthemis arvensis	Corn Chamomile
cotula	Stinking C.
tinctoria	Yellow C.
Anthoxanthum odoratum	Sweet Vernal-grass
puelii	Annual V.
Anthriscus caucalis	Bur Chervil
cerefolium	Garden C.
sylvestris	Cow Parsley
Anthyllis vulneraria	Kidney Vetch
Antirrhinum majus	Snapdragon
orontium *see* Misopates o.	
Apera interrupta	Dense Silky-bent
spica-venti	Loose S.
Aphanes arvensis	Parsley-piert
microcarpa	Slender P.
Apium graveolens	Wild Celery
inundatum	Lesser Marshwort
nodiflorum	Fool's Water-cress
repens	Creeping Marshwort
Aquilegia vulgaris	Columbine
Arabidopsis thaliana	Thale Cress
Arabis alpina	Alpine Rock-cress
brownii	Fringed R.
caucasica	Garden Arabis
hirsuta	Hairy Rock-cress
scabra	Bristol R.
stricta *see* A.scabra	
turrita	Tower Cress
Arbutus unedo	Strawberry-tree
Arctium lappa	Greater Burdock
minus	Lesser B.
Arctostaphylos uva-ursi	Bearberry

Arctous alpinus	Alpine Bearberry
Arenaria balearica	Mossy Sandwort
ciliata subsp. hibernica	Fringed S.
gothica *see* A.norvegica	
subsp. anglica	
leptoclados	Slender S.
norvegica subsp. anglica	English S.
norvegica subsp. norvegica	Arctic S.
serpyllifolia	Thyme-leaved S.
Aristolochia clematitis	Birthwort
Armeria arenaria	Jersey Thrift
maritima	Thrift
Armoracia rusticana	Horse-radish
Arnoseris minima	Lamb's Succory
Arrhenatherum elatius	False Oat-grass
Artemisia absinthium	Wormwood
campestris	Field W.
maritima	Sea W.
norvegica	Norwegian Mugwort
stellerana	Hoary M.
verlotorum	Chinese M.
vulgaris	Mugwort
Arum italicum	Italian Lords-and-Ladies
maculatum	Lords-and-Ladies
Asarum europaeum	Asarabacca
Asparagus officinalis	Wild Asparagus
Asperugo procumbens	Madwort
Asperula cynanchica	Squinancywort
taurina	Pink Woodruff
Asplenium adiantum-nigrum	Black Spleenwort
billotii	Lanceolate S.
marinum	Sea S.
obovatum *see* A.billotii	
ruta-muraria	Wall-rue
septentrionale	Forked Spleenwort
trichomanes	Maidenhair S.
viride	Green S.

Aster linosyris

Aster linosyris *see* Crinitaria
  linosyris
  novi-belgii   Michaelmas-daisy
  tripolium   Sea Aster

Astragalus alpinus   Alpine Milk-vetch
  danicus   Purple M.
  glycyphyllos   Wild Liquorice

Astrantia major   Astrantia

Athyrium alpestre *see*
    A.distentifolium
  distentifolium   Alpine Lady-fern
  filix-femina   Lady-fern

Atriplex glabriuscula   Babington's Orache
  halimus   Shrubby O.
  hastata   Spear-leaved O.
  hortensis   Garden O.
  laciniata   Frosted O.
  littoralis   Grass-leaved O.
  patula   Common O.

Atropa belladonna   Deadly Nightshade

Avena fatua   Wild-oat
  ludoviciana   Winter W.
  strigosa   Bristle Oat

Azolla filiculoides   Water Fern

Baldellia ranunculoides   Lesser Water-plantain

Ballota nigra   Black Horehound

Barbarea intermedia   Medium-flowered Winter-
                                   cress
  stricta   Small-flowered W.
  verna   American W.
  vulgaris   Winter-cress

Bartsia alpina   Alpine Bartsia

Bellis perennis   Daisy

Berberis vulgaris   Barberry

Berteroa incana   Hoary Alison

14

Berula erecta	Lesser Water-parsnip
Beta vulgaris subsp. maritima	Sea Beet
Betonica officinalis	Betony
Betula nana	Dwarf Birch
pendula	Silver B.
pubescens	Downy B.
Bidens cernua	Nodding Bur-marigold
frondosa	Beggarticks
tripartita	Trifid Bur-marigold
Blackstonia perfoliata	Yellow-wort
Blechnum spicant	Hard Fern
Blysmus compressus	Flat-sedge
rufus	Saltmarsh F.
Borago officinalis	Borage
Botrychium lunaria	Moonwort
Brachypodium pinnatum	Tor-grass
sylvaticum	False Brome
Brassica oleracea	Wild Cabbage
napus	Rape
nigra	Black Mustard
rapa	Wild Turnip
Briza maxima	Great Quaking-grass
media	Quaking-grass
minor	Lesser Q.
Bromus arvensis	Field Brome
benekenii	Lesser Hairy-brome
carinatus	California Brome
commutatus	Meadow B.
diandrus	Great B.
erectus	Upright B.
ferronii	Least Soft-brome
inermis	Hungarian Brome
interruptus	Interrupted B.
lepidus	Slender Soft-brome
madritensis	Compact Brome
mollis	Soft-brome

Bromus—*continued*

racemosus	Smooth Brome
ramosus	Hairy-brome
secalinus	Rye Brome
sterilis	Barren Brome
tectorum	Drooping B.
thominii	Lesser Soft-brome
unioloides *see* B.willdenowii	
willdenowii	Rescue Brome

Bryonia dioica	White Bryony
Buddleja davidii	Butterfly-bush
Bunias orientalis	Warty Cabbage
Bunium bulbocastanum	Great Pignut

Bupleurum baldense	Small Hare's-ear
falcatum	Sickle-leaved H.
fruticosum	Shrubby H.
lancifolium	False Thorow-wax
rotundifolium	Thorow-wax
tenuissimum	Slender Hare's-ear

Butomus umbellatus	Flowering-rush
Buxus sempervirens	Box

Cakile maritima	Sea Rocket

Calamagrostis canescens	Purple Small-reed
epigejos	Wood S.
scotica	Scottish S.
stricta	Narrow S.

Calamintha ascendens	Common Calamint
nepeta	Lesser C.
sylvatica	Wood C.

Calendula arvensis	Field Marigold
officinalis	Pot M.

Callitriche hermaphroditica	Autumnal Water-starwort
intermedia	Intermediate W.
obtusangula	Blunt-fruited W.
platycarpa	Various-leaved W.
stagnalis	Common W.
truncata	Short-leaved W.

Calluna vulgaris	Heather
Caltha palustris	Marsh-marigold
Calystegia dahurica *see* C.pulchra	
pulchra	Hairy Bindweed
sepium	Hedge B.
sepium subsp. pulchra *see* C.pulchra	
sepium subsp. silvatica *see* C.sylvatica	
soldanella	Sea Bindweed
sylvatica	Large B.
Camelina sativa	Gold-of-pleasure
Campanula glomerata	Clustered Bellflower
latifolia	Giant B.
medium	Canterbury-bells
patula	Spreading Bellflower
persicifolia	Peach-leaved B.
rapunculoides	Creeping B.
rapunculus	Rampion B.
rotundifolia	Harebell
trachelium	Nettle-leaved Bellflower
Capsella bursa-pastoris	Shepherd's-purse
Cardamine amara	Large Bitter-cress
bulbifera	Coralroot
flexuosa	Wavy Bitter-cress
hirsuta	Hairy B.
impatiens	Narrow-leaved B.
pratensis	Cuckooflower
Cardaminopsis petraea	Northern Rock-cress
Cardaria draba	Hoary Cress
Carduus acanthoides	Welted Thistle
nutans	Musk T.
pycnocephalus	Plymouth T.
tenuiflorus	Slender T.
Carex acuta	Slender Tufted-sedge
acutiformis	Lesser Pond-sedge
appropinquata	Fibrous Tussock-sedge
aquatilis	Water Sedge

Carex—*continued*

arenaria	Sand Sedge
atrata	Black Alpine-sedge
atrofusca	Scorched A.
bigelowii	Stiff Sedge
binervis	Green-ribbed S.
buxbaumii	Club S.
capillaris	Hair S.
caryophyllea	Spring-sedge
chordorrhiza	String Sedge
curta	White S.
demissa	Common Yellow-sedge
depauperata	Starved Wood-sedge
diandra	Lesser Tussock-sedge
digitata	Fingered Sedge
dioica	Dioecious S.
distans	Distant S.
disticha	Brown S.
divisa	Divided S.
divulsa	Grey S.
echinata	Star S.
elata	Tufted-sedge
elongata	Elongated Sedge
ericetorum	Rare Spring-sedge
extensa	Long-bracted Sedge
filiformis	Downy-fruited S.
flacca	Glaucous S.
flava	Large Yellow-sedge
hirta	Hairy Sedge
hostiana	Tawny S.
humilis	Dwarf S.
lachenalii	Hare's-foot S.
laevigata	Smooth-stalked S.
lasiocarpa	Slender S.
lepidocarpa	Long-stalked Yellow-sedge
limosa	Bog-sedge
maritima	Curved Sedge
microglochin	Bristle S.
montana	Soft-leaved S.
muricata	Prickly S.
nigra	Common S.
norvegica	Close-headed Alpine-sedge
ornithopoda	Bird's-foot Sedge
otrubae	False Fox-sedge
ovalis	Oval Sedge
pallescens	Pale S.
panicea	Carnation S.
paniculata	Greater Tussock-sedge
pauciflora	Few-flowered Sedge

Carex—*continued*
paupercula	Tall Bog-sedge
pendula	Pendulous Sedge
pilulifera	Pill S.
pseudocyperus	Cyperus S.
pulicaris	Flea S.
punctata	Dotted S.
rariflora	Mountain Bog-sedge
recta	Estuarine Sedge
remota	Remote S.
riparia	Greater Pond-sedge
rostrata	Bottle Sedge
rupestris	Rock S.
saxatilis	Russet S.
serotina	Small-fruited Yellow-sedge
spicata	Spiked Sedge
stenolepis	Mountain Bladder-sedge
strigosa	Thin-spiked Wood-sedge
sylvatica	Wood-sedge
vaginata	Sheathed Sedge
vesicaria	Bladder-sedge
vulpina	True Fox-sedge

Carlina vulgaris — Carline Thistle

Carpinus betulus — Hornbeam

Carpobrotus edulis — Hottentot-fig

Carum carvi — Caraway
  verticillatum — Whorled C.

Castanea sativa — Sweet Chestnut

Catabrosa aquatica — Whorl-grass

Catapodium marinum — Sea Fern-grass
  rigidum — Fern-grass

Caucalis latifolia — Greater Bur-parsley
  platycarpos — Small B.

Centaurea aspera — Rough Star-thistle
  calcitrapa — Red S.
  cyanus — Cornflower
  jacea — Brown Knapweed
  montana — Perennial Cornflower
  nemoralis — Slender Knapweed

19

Centaurea—*continued*
  nigra   Common Knapweed
  nigra subsp. nemoralis *see*
     C.nemoralis
  paniculata   Jersey K.
  scabiosa   Greater K.
  solstitialis   Yellow Star-thistle

Centaurium capitatum   Tufted Centaury
  erythraea   Common C.
  latifolium   Broad-leaved C.
  littorale   Seaside C.
  portense *see* C.scilloides
  pulchellum   Lesser C.
  scilloides   Perennial C.
  tenuiflorum   Slender C.

Centranthus ruber   Red Valerian

Cephalanthera damasonium   White Helleborine
  longifolia   Narrow-leaved H.
  rubra   Red H.

Cerastium alpinum   Alpine Mouse-ear
  arcticum   Arctic M.
  arvense   Field M.
  atrovirens *see* C.diffusum
  brachypetalum   Grey M.
  cerastoides   Starwort M.
  diffusum   Sea M.
  glomeratum   Sticky M.
  holosteoides   Common M.
  nigrescens   Shetland M.
  pumilum   Dwarf M.
  semidecandrum   Little M.
  tomentosum   Snow-in-Summer

Ceratochloa carinata *see*
     Bromus carinatus
  unioloides *see* Bromus
     willdenowii

Ceratophyllum demersum   Rigid Hornwort
  submersum   Soft H.

Ceterach officinarum   Rustyback

Chaenorhinum minus   Small Toadflax

Chaerophyllum aureum — Golden Chervil
   temulentum — Rough C.

Chamaemelum nobile — Chamomile

Chamaenerion angustifolium
   see Epilobium a.

Chamaepericlymenum — Dwarf Cornel
   suecicum

Cheiranthus cheiri — Wallflower

Chelidonium majus — Greater Celandine

Chenopodium album — Fat-hen
   bonus-henricus — Good-King-Henry
   capitatum — Strawberry-blite
   ficifolium — Fig-leaved Goosefoot
   glaucum — Oak-leaved G.
   hybridum — Maple-leaved G.
   murale — Nettle-leaved G.
   opulifolium — Grey G.
   polyspermum — Many-seeded G.
   rubrum — Red G.
   urbicum — Upright G.
   vulvaria — Stinking G.

Cherleria sedoides — Cyphel

Chrysanthemum
   leucanthemum *see*
      Leucanthemum
      vulgare
   maximum *see*
      Leucanthemum m.
   parthenium *see*
      Tanacetum p.
   segetum — Corn Marigold
   vulgare *see* Tanacetum v.

Chrysosplenium alternifolium — Alternate-leaved Golden-
                         saxifrage
   oppositifolium — Opposite-leaved G.

Cicendia filiformis — Yellow Centaury

Cicerbita alpina — Alpine Sow-thistle
   macrophylla — Blue S.

Cichorium intybus	Chicory
Cicuta virosa	Cowbane
Circaea alpina	Alpine Enchanter's-nightshade
intermedia	Upland E.
lutetiana	Enchanter's-nightshade
Cirsium acaule	Dwarf Thistle
acaulon *see* C.acaule	
arvense	Creeping T.
dissectum	Meadow T.
eriophorum	Woolly T.
heterophyllum	Melancholy T.
oleraceum	Cabbage T.
palustre	Marsh T.
tuberosum	Tuberous T.
vulgare	Spear T.
Cladium mariscus	Great Fen-sedge
Clematis vitalba	Traveller's-joy
Clinopodium vulgare	Wild Basil
Cochlearia alpina	Alpine Scurvygrass
anglica	English S.
danica	Danish S.
officinalis	Common S.
officinalis subsp. anglica *see* C.anglica	
scotica	Scottish S.
Coeloglossum viride	Frog Orchid
Colchicum autumnale	Meadow Saffron
Colutea arborescens	Bladder-senna
Conium maculatum	Hemlock
Conopodium majus	Pignut
Conringia orientalis	Hare's-ear Mustard
Convallaria majalis	Lily-of-the-valley
Convolvulus arvensis	Field Bindweed

Conyza canadensis	Canadian Fleabane
Corallorhiza trifida	Coralroot Orchid
Coriandrum sativum	Coriander
Cornus sanguinea *see* Swida s.	
Coronilla varia	Crown Vetch
Coronopus didymus squamatus	Lesser Swine-cress Swine-cress
Corrigiola litoralis	Strapwort
Cortaderia selloana	Pampas-grass
Corydalis claviculata lutea	Climbing Corydalis Yellow C.
Corylus avellana	Hazel
Corynephorus canescens	Grey Hair-grass
Cotoneaster horizontalis integerrimus microphyllus simonsii	Wall Cotoneaster Wild C. Small-leaved C. Himalayan C.
Cotula coronopifolia	Buttonweed
Crambe maritima	Sea-kale
Crassula tillaea	Mossy Stonecrop
Crataegus laevigata monogyna oxyacanthoides *see* C.laevigata	Midland Hawthorn Hawthorn
Crepis biennis capillaris foetida mollis paludosa setosa vesicaria subsp. taraxacifolia	Rough Hawk's-beard Smooth H. Stinking H. Northern H. Marsh H. Bristly H. Beaked H.
Crinitaria linosyris	Goldilocks Aster
Crithmum maritimum	Rock Samphire

Crocosmia × crocosmiflora	Montbretia
Crocus nudiflorus	Autumn Crocus
purpureus	Spring C.
sativus	Saffron C.
Cruciata chersonensis *see*	
C.laevipes	
laevipes	Crosswort
Cryptogramma crispa	Parsley Fern
Cucubalus baccifer	Berry Catchfly
Cuscuta epilinum	Flax Dodder
epithymum	Dodder
europaea	Greater D.
Cyclamen hederifolium	Cyclamen
Cymbalaria muralis	Ivy-leafed Toadflax
Cynodon dactylon	Bermuda-grass
Cynoglossum germanicum	Green Hound's-tongue
officinale	Hound's-tongue
Cynosurus cristatus	Crested Dog's-tail
echinatus	Rough D.
Cyperus fuscus	Brown Galingale
longus	Galingale
Cypripedium calceolus	Lady's-slipper
Cystopteris fragilis	Brittle Bladder-fern
montana	Mountain B.
Daboecia cantabrica	St. Dabeoc's Heath
Dactylis glomerata	Cock's-foot
Dactylorchis *see* Dactylorhiza	
majalis *see* Dactylorhiza	
kerryensis	
Dactylorhiza fuchsii	Common Spotted-orchid
incarnata	Early Marsh-orchid

Dactylorhiza—*continued*
    kerryensis   Irish Marsh-orchid
    maculata   Heath Spotted-orchid
    praetermissa   Southern Marsh-orchid
    purpurella   Northern M.
    traunsteineri   Narrow-leaved M.

Damasonium alisma   Starfruit

Daphne laureola   Spurge-laurel
    mezereum   Mezereon

Datura stramonium   Thorn-apple

Daucus carota   Wild Carrot

Delphinium ambiguum   Larkspur

Dentaria bulbifera *see*
    Cardamine b.

Deschampsia alpina   Alpine Hair-grass
    cespitosa   Tufted H.
    flexuosa   Wavy H.
    setacea   Bog H.

Descurainia sophia   Flixweed

Dianthus armeria   Deptford Pink
    barbatus   Sweet-William
    caryophyllus   Clove Pink
    deltoides   Maiden P.
    gallicus   Jersey P.
    gratianopolitanus   Cheddar P.
    plumarius   Pink

Diapensia lapponica   Diapensia

Digitalis purpurea   Foxglove

Digitaria ischaemum   Smooth Finger-grass
    sanguinalis   Hairy F.

Diplotaxis erucoides   White Rocket
    muralis   Annual Wall-rocket
    tenuifolia   Perennial W.

Dipsacus fullonum   Teasel
    pilosus   Small T.

Doronicum pardalianches	Leopard's-bane
plantagineum	Plantain-leaved L.
Draba aizoides	Yellow Whitlowgrass
incana	Hoary W.
muralis	Wall W.
norvegica	Rock W.
Drosera anglica	Great Sundew
intermedia	Oblong-leaved S.
rotundifolia	Round-leaved S.
Dryas octopetala	Mountain Avens
Dryopteris aemula	Hay-scented Buckler-fern
borreri *see* D.pseudomas	
carthusiana	Narrow B.
cristata	Crested B.
dilatata	Broad B.
filix-mas	Male-fern
lanceolatocristata *see*	
D.carthusianà	
pseudomas	Scaly M.
villarii	Rigid Buckler-fern
Echinochloa crus-galli	Cockspur
Echium lycopsis	Purple Viper's-bugloss
vulgare	Viper's-bugloss
Elatine hexandra	Six-stamened Waterwort
hydropiper	Eight-stamened W.
Eleocharis acicularis	Needle Spike-rush
austriaca	Northern S.
multicaulis	Many-stalked S.
palustris	Common S.
parvula	Dwarf S.
quinqueflora	Few-flowered S.
uniglumis	Slender S.
Eleogiton fluitans *see*	
Scirpus f.	
Elodea canadensis	Canadian Waterweed
Elymus arenarius	Lyme-grass

Empetrum hermaphroditum	Mountain Crowberry
nigrum	Crowberry
Endymion hispanicus	Spanish Bluebell
non-scriptus	Bluebell
Epilobium adenocaulon	American Willowherb
adnatum *see* E.tetragonum	
alsinifolium	Chickweed W.
anagallidifolium	Alpine W.
angustifolium	Rosebay W.
hirsutum	Great W.
lanceolatum	Spear-leaved W.
montanum	Broad-leaved W.
nerterioides	New Zealand W.
obscurum	Short-fruited W.
palustre	Marsh W.
parviflorum	Hoary W.
roseum	Pale W.
tetragonum	Square-stalked W.
Epipactis atrorubens	Dark-red Helleborine
dunensis	Dune H.
helleborine	Broad-leaved H.
leptochila	Narrow-lipped H.
palustris	Marsh H.
phyllanthes	Green-flowered H.
purpurata	Violet H.
Epipogium aphyllum	Ghost Orchid
Equisetum arvense	Field Horsetail
fluviatile	Water H.
hyemale	Rough H.
palustre	Marsh H.
pratense	Shady H.
sylvaticum	Wood H.
telmateia	Great H.
variegatum	Variegated H.
Eranthis hyemalis	Winter Aconite
Erica ciliaris	Dorset Heath
cinerea	Bell Heather
erigena	Irish Heath
mackaiana	Mackay's H.
mediterranea *see* E.erigena	
terminalis	Corsican H.
tetralix	Cross-leaved H.
vagans	Cornish H.

27

Erigeron acer	Blue Fleabane
borealis	Alpine F.
mucronatus	Mexican F.
Erinus alpinus	Fairy Foxglove
Eriocaulon aquaticum	Pipewort
septangulare *see*	
E.aquaticum	
Eriophorum angustifolium	Common Cottongrass
gracile	Slender C.
latifolium	Broad-leaved C.
vaginatum	Hare's-tail C.
Erodium cicutarium	Common Stork's-bill
glutinosum	Sticky S.
maritimum	Sea S.
moschatum	Musk S.
Erophila spathulata	Round-podded Whitlowgrass
verna	Common W.
Erucastrum gallicum	Hairy Rocket
Eryngium campestre	Field Eryngo
maritimum	Sea-holly
Erysimum cheiranthoides	Treacle Mustard
Eschscholzia californica	Californian Poppy
Euonymus europaeus	Spindle
Eupatorium cannabinum	Hemp-agrimony
Euphorbia amygdaloides	Wood Spurge
corallioides	Coral S.
cyparissias	Cypress S.
dulcis	Sweet S.
esula	Leafy S.
exigua	Dwarf S.
helioscopia	Sun S.
hyberna	Irish S.
lathyrus	Caper S.
paralias	Sea S.
peplis	Purple S.
peplus	Petty S.
platyphyllos	Broad-leaved S.

28

Euphorbia—*continued*
  pilosa *see* E.villosa
  portlandica — Portland Spurge
  serrulata — Upright S.
  stricta *see* E.serrulata
  uralensis — Twiggy S.
  villosa — Hairy S.

Euphrasia officinalis — Eyebright
  salisburgensis — Irish E.

Exaculum pusillum — Guernsey Centaury

Fagopyrum esculentum — Buckwheat

Fagus sylvatica — Beech

Falcaria vulgaris — Longleaf

Festuca altissima — Wood Fescue
  arundinacea — Tall F.
  gigantea — Giant F.
  glauca — Blue F.
  heterophylla — Various-leaved F.
  juncifolia — Rush-leaved F.
  longifolia — Hard F.
  ovina — Sheep's-fescue
  ovina subsp.tenuifolia *see* F.tenuifolia
  pratensis — Meadow Fescue
  rubra — Red F.
  tenuifolia — Fine-leaved Sheep's-fescue
  vivipara — Viviparous Fescue

Ficus carica — Fig

Filago apiculata *see* F.lutescens
  gallica — Narrow-leaved Cudweed
  germanica *see* F.vulgaris
  lutescens — Red-tipped C.
  minima — Small C.
  pyramidata — Broad-leaved C.
  spathulata *see* F.pyramidata
  vulgaris — Common C.

Filipendula ulmaria — Meadowsweet
  vulgaris — Dropwort

Foeniculum vulgare	Fennel
Fragaria ananassa	Garden Strawberry
vesca	Wild S.
Frangula alnus	Alder Buckthorn
Frankenia laevis	Sea-heath
Fraxinus excelsior	Ash
Fritillaria meleagris	Fritillary
Fuchsia magellanica	Fuchsia
Fumaria bastardii	Tall Ramping-fumitory
capreolata	White R.
densiflora	Dense-flowered Fumitory
micrantha *see* F.densiflora	
muralis subsp. boraei	Common Ramping-fumitory
officinalis	Common Fumitory
parviflora	Fine-leaved F.
purpurea	Purple Ramping-fumitory
vaillantii	Few-flowered Fumitory
Gagea lutea	Yellow Star-of-Bethlehem
Galanthus nivalis	Snowdrop
Galega officinalis	Goat's-rue

Galeobdolon luteum *see*
    Lamiastrum
    galeobdolon	

Galeopsis angustifolia	Red Hemp-nettle
segetum	Downy H.
speciosa	Large-flowered H.
tetrahit	Common H.
Galinsoga ciliata	Shaggy Soldier
parviflora	Gallant S.
Galium aparine	Cleavers
boreale	Northern Bedstraw
cruciata *see* Cruciata laevipes	
debile	Slender Marsh-bedstraw

Galium—*continued*

mollugo	Hedge Bedstraw
odoratum	Woodruff
palustre	Common Marsh-bedstraw
parisiense	Wall Bedstraw
pumilum	Slender B.
saxatile	Heath B.
spurium	False Cleavers
sterneri	Limestone Bedstraw
tricornutum	Corn Cleavers
uliginosum	Fen Bedstraw
verum	Lady's B.

Gastridium ventricosum	Nit-grass

Gaultheria shallon	Shallon

Genista anglica	Petty Whin
pilosa	Hairy Greenweed
tinctoria	Dyer's G.

Gentiana nivalis	Alpine Gentian
pneumonanthe	Marsh G.
verna	Spring G.

Gentianella amarella	Autumn Gentian
anglica	Early G.
campestris	Field G.
germanica	Chiltern G.
uliginosa	Dune G.

Geranium columbinum	Long-stalked Crane's-bill
dissectum	Cut-leaved C.
endressii	French C.
lucidum	Shining C.
molle	Dove's-foot C.
nodosum	Knotted C.
phaeum	Dusky C.
pratense	Meadow C.
purpureum	Little-Robin
pusillum	Small-flowered Crane's-bill
pyrenaicum	Hedgerow C.
robertianum	Herb-Robert
rotundifolium	Round-leaved Crane's-bill
sanguineum	Bloody C.
sylvaticum	Wood C.
versicolor	Pencilled C.

Geum rivale	Water Avens
urbanum	Wood A.

Gladiolus illyricus	Wild Gladiolus
Glaucium flavum	Yellow Horned-poppy
Glaux maritima	Sea-milkwort
Glechoma hederacea	Ground-ivy
Glyceria declinata	Small Sweet-grass
fluitans	Floating S.
maxima	Reed S.
plicata	Plicate S.
Gnaphalium luteoalbum	Jersey Cudweed
norvegicum	Highland C.
supinum	Dwarf C.
sylvaticum	Heath C.
uliginosum	Marsh C.
Goodyera repens	Creeping Lady's-tresses
Groenlandia densa	Opposite-leaved Pondweed
Gymnadenia conopsea	Fragrant Orchid
Gymnocarpium dryopteris	Oak Fern
robertianum	Limestone F.
Halimione portulacoides	Sea-purslane
Hammarbya paludosa	Bog Orchid
Hedera helix	Ivy
Helianthemum apenninum	White Rock-rose
canum	Hoary R.
chamaecistus	Common R.
Helictotrichon pratense	Meadow Oat-grass
pubescens	Downy O.
Helleborus foetidus	Stinking Hellebore
viridis	Green H.
Helxine soleirolii *see*	
Soleirolia s.	
Heracleum mantegazzianum	Giant Hogweed
sphondylium	Hogweed

Herminium monorchis	Musk Orchid
Hermodactylus tuberosus	Snake's-head Iris
Herniaria ciliolata	Fringed Rupturewort
glabra	Smooth R.
Hesperis matronalis	Dame's-violet
Hieracium murorum	Hawkweed
pilosella	Mouse-ear H.
Hierochloe odorata	Holy-grass
Himantoglossum hircinum	Lizard Orchid
Hippocrepis comosa	Horseshoe Vetch
Hippophae rhamnoides	Sea-buckthorn
Hippuris vulgaris	Mare's-tail
Hirschfeldia incana	Hoary Mustard
Holcus lanatus	Yorkshire-fog
mollis	Creeping Soft-grass
Holoschoenus vulgaris *see* Scirpus holoschoenus	
Homogyne alpina	Purple Coltsfoot
Honkenya peploides	Sea Sandwort
Hordelymus europaeus	Wood Barley
Hordeum jubatum	Foxtail Barley
marinum	Sea B.
murinum	Wall B.
secalinum	Meadow B.
Hornungia petraea	Hutchinsia
Hottonia palustris	Water-violet
Humulus lupulus	Hop
Hydrocharis morsus-ranae	Frogbit
Hydrocotyle vulgaris	Marsh Pennywort

Hymenophyllum tunbrigense	Tunbridge Filmy-fern
wilsonii	Wilson's F.
Hyoscyamus niger	Henbane
Hypericum androsaemum	Tutsan
calycinum	Rose-of-Sharon
canadense	Irish St. John's-wort
elatum *see* H.inodorum	
elodes	Marsh S.
hircinum	Stinking Tutsan
hirsutum	Hairy St. John's-wort
humifusum	Trailing S.
inodorum	Tall Tutsan
linarifolium	Flax-leaved St. John's-wort
maculatum	Imperforate S.
montanum	Pale S.
perforatum	Perforate S.
pulchrum	Slender S.
tetrapterum	Square-stalked S.
undulatum	Wavy S.
Hypochoeris glabra	Smooth Cat's-ear
maculata	Spotted C.
radicata	Cat's-ear
Hyssopus officinalis	Hyssop
Iberis amara	Wild Candytuft
Ilex aquifolium	Holly
Illecebrum verticillatum	Coral-necklace
Impatiens capensis	Orange Balsam
glandulifera	Indian B.
noli-tangere	Touch-me-not B.
parviflora	Small B.
Inula conyza	Ploughman's-spikenard
crithmoides	Golden Samphire
helenium	Elecampane
salicina	Irish Fleabane
Iris foetidissima	Stinking Iris
pseudacorus	Yellow I.
spuria	Blue I.
versicolor	Purple I.

Isatis tinctoria	Woad
Isoetes echinospora	Spring Quillwort
histrix	Land Q.
lacustris	Quillwort

Isolepis cernua *see*
    Scirpus cernuus
  setacea *see* Scirpus setaceus

Jasione montana	Sheep's-bit
Juglans regia	Walnut
Juncus acutiflorus	Sharp-flowered Rush
acutus	Sharp R.
alpinoarticulatus	Alpine R.
articulatus	Jointed R.
balticus	Baltic Rush
biglumis	Two-flowered R.
bufonius	Toad R.
bulbosus	Bulbous R.
capitatus	Dwarf R.
castaneus	Chestnut R.
compressus	Round-fruited R.

  conglomeratus *see*
    J.subuliflorus

effusus	Soft R.
filiformis	Thread R.
gerardii	Saltmarsh R.
inflexus	Hard R.
maritimus	Sea R.
mutabilis	Pigmy R.
nodulosus	Marshall's R.
squarrosus	Heath R.
subnodulosus	Blunt-flowered R.
subuliflorus	Compact R.
tenuis	Slender R.
trifidus	Three-leaved R.
triglumis	Three-flowered R.
Juniperus communis	Juniper
Kickxia elatine	Sharp-leaved Fluellen
spuria	Round-leaved F.
Knautia arvensis	Field Scabious

Kobresia simpliciuscula	False Sedge
Koeleria cristata	Crested Hair-grass
vallesiana	Somerset H.
Koenigia islandica	Iceland-purslane
Kohlrauschia prolifera *see*	
Petrorhagia nanteuilii	
Laburnum anagyroides	Laburnum
Lactuca saligna	Least Lettuce
serriola	Prickly L.
virosa	Great L.
Lagurus ovatus	Hare's-tail
Lamiastrum galeobdolon	Yellow Archangel
Lamium album	White Dead-nettle
amplexicaule	Henbit D.
hybridum	Cut-leaved D.
maculatum	Spotted D.
moluccellifolium	Northern D.
purpureum	Red D.
Lapsana communis	Nipplewort
Larix decidua	European Larch
Lathraea clandestina	Purple Toothwort
squamaria	Toothwort
Lathyrus aphaca	Yellow Vetchling
hirsutus	Hairy V.
japonicus	Sea Pea
latifolius	Broad-leaved Everlasting-pea
montanus	Bitter Vetch
niger	Black Pea
nissolia	Grass Vetchling
palustris	Marsh Pea
pratensis	Meadow Vetchling
sylvestris	Narrow-leaved Everlasting-pea
tuberosus	Tuberous Pea
Lavatera arborea	Tree-mallow
cretica	Smaller T.

Ledum groenlandicum	Labrador-tea
Leersia oryzoides	Cut-grass
Legousia hybrida	Venus's-looking-glass
Lemna gibba	Fat Duckweed
minor	Common D.
polyrrhiza	Greater D.
trisulca	Ivy-leaved D.
Leontodon autumnalis	Autumn Hawkbit
hispidus	Rough H.
taraxacoides	Lesser H.
Leonurus cardiaca	Motherwort
Lepidium campestre	Field Pepperwort
graminifolium	Tall P.
heterophyllum	Smith's P.
latifolium	Dittander
neglectum	Least Pepperwort
ruderale	Narrow-leaved P.
sativum	Garden Cress
Leucanthemum maximum	Shasta Daisy
vulgare	Oxeye D.
Leucojum aestivum	Summer Snowflake
vernum	Spring S.
Leucorchis albida *see* Pseudorchis a.	
Leycesteria formosa	Himalayan Honeysuckle
Ligusticum scoticum	Scots Lovage
Ligustrum ovalifolium	Garden Privet
vulgare	Wild P.
Lilium martagon	Martagon Lily
pyrenaicum	Pyrenean L.
Limonium auriculae-ursifolium	Alderney Sea-lavender
bellidifolium	Matted S.
binervosum	Rock S.
humile	Lax-flowered S.
vulgare	Common S.

Limosella aquatica	Mudwort
australis	Welsh M.
subulata *see* L.australis	
Linaria arenaria	Sand Toadflax
pelisseriana	Jersey T.
purpurea	Purple T.
repens	Pale T.
supina	Prostrate T.
vulgaris	Common T.
Linnaea borealis	Twinflower
Linum anglicum	Perennial Flax
bienne	Pale F.
catharticum	Fairy F.
usitatissimum	Flax
Liparis loeselii	Fen Orchid
Listera cordata	Lesser Twayblade
ovata	Common T.
Lithospermum arvense	Field Gromwell
officinale	Common G.
purpurocaeruleum	Purple G.
Littorella uniflora	Shoreweed
Lloydia serotina	Snowdon Lily
Lobelia dortmanna	Water Lobelia
urens	Heath L.
Lobularia maritima	Sweet Alison
Loiseleuria procumbens	Trailing Azalea
Lolium multiflorum	Italian Rye-grass
perenne	Perennial R.
temulentum	Darnel
Lonicera caprifolium	Perfoliate Honeysuckle
periclymenum	Honeysuckle
xylosteum	Fly H.
Lotus angustissimus	Slender Bird's-foot-trefoil
corniculatus	Common B.
hispidus *see* L.subuliflorus	

pedunculatus *see*
    L.uliginosus
subuliflorus   Hairy Bird's-foot-trefoil
tenuis   Narrow-leaved B.
uliginosus   Greater B.

Ludwigia palustris   Hampshire-purslane

Lunaria annua   Honesty

Lupinus arboreus   Tree Lupin
  nootkatensis   Nootka L.

Luronium natans   Floating Water-plantain

Luzula arcuata   Curved Wood-rush
  campestris   Field W.
  forsteri   Southern W.
  luzuloides   White W.
  multiflora   Heath W.
  pallescens   Fen W.
  pilosa   Hairy W.
  spicata   Spiked W.
  sylvatica   Great W.

Lychnis alpina   Alpine Catchfly
  flos-cuculi   Ragged-Robin
  viscaria   Sticky Catchfly

Lycium barbarum   Duke of Argyll's Teaplant
  chinense   China T.
  halimifolium *see*
      L.barbarum

Lycopodium alpinum   Alpine Clubmoss
  annotinum   Interrupted C.
  clavatum   Stag's-horn C.
  inundatum   Marsh C.
  selago   Fir C.

Lycopsis arvensis   Bugloss

Lycopus europaeus   Gipsywort

Lysimachia ciliata   Fringed Loosestrife
  nemorum   Yellow Pimpernel
  nummularia   Creeping-Jenny
  punctata   Dotted Loosestrife

Lysimachia—*continued*
  terrestris   Lake Loosestrife
  thyrsiflora   Tufted L.
  vulgaris   Yellow L.

Lythrum hyssopifolia   Grass-poly
  salicaria   Purple-loosestrife

Mahonia aquifolium   Oregon-grape

Maianthemum bifolium   May Lily

Malus sylvestris   Crab Apple

Malva moschata   Musk Mallow
  neglecta   Dwarf M.
  parviflora   Least M.
  pusilla   Small M.
  sylvestris   Common M.
  verticillata   Chinese M.

Marrubium vulgare   White Horehound

Matricaria matricarioides Pineappleweed
  recutita   Scented Mayweed

Matthiola incana   Hoary Stock
  sinuata   Sea S.

Meconopsis cambrica   Welsh Poppy

Medicago arabica   Spotted Medick
  falcata   Sickle M.
  lupulina   Black M.
  minima   Bur M.
  polymorpha   Toothed M.
  sativa   Lucerne

Melampyrum arvense   Field Cow-wheat
  cristatum   Crested C.
  pratense   Common C.
  sylvaticum   Small C.

Melica nutans   Mountain Melick
  uniflora   Wood M.

Melilotus alba   White Melilot
  altissima   Tall M.

Melilotus—*continued*	
indica	Small Melilot
officinalis	Ribbed M.
Melissa officinalis	Balm
Melittis melissophyllum	Bastard Balm
Mentha aquatica	Water Mint
arvensis	Corn M.
longifolia	Horse M.
pulegium	Pennyroyal
requienii	Corsican Mint
rotundifolia	Round-leaved M.
spicata	Spear M.
Menyanthes trifoliata	Bogbean
Mercurialis annua	Annual Mercury
perennis	Dog's M.
Mertensia maritima	Oysterplant
Mespilus germanica	Medlar
Meum athamanticum	Spignel
Mibora minima	Early Sand-grass
Milium effusum	Wood Millet
scabrum	Early M.
Mimulus guttatus	Monkeyflower
luteus	Blood-drop-emlets
moschatus	Musk
Minuartia hybrida	Fine-leaved Sandwort
rubella	Mountain S.
stricta	Teesdale S.
verna	Spring S.
Misopates orontium	Lesser Snapdragon
Moehringia trinervia	Three-nerved Sandwort
Moenchia erecta	Upright Chickweed
Molinia caerulea	Purple Moor-grass
Moneses uniflora	One-flowered Wintergreen

41

Monotropa hypopitys	Yellow Bird's-nest
Montia fontana	Blinks
perfoliata	Springbeauty
sibirica	Pink Purslane
Muscari atlanticum	Grape Hyacinth
Mycelis muralis	Wall Lettuce
Myosotis alpestris	Alpine Forget-me-not
arvensis	Field F.
brevifolia *see* M.stolonifera	
caespitosa	Tufted F.
discolor	Changing F.
ramosissima	Early F.
scorpioides	Water F.
secunda	Creeping F.
sicula	Jersey F.
stolonifera	Pale F.
sylvatica	Wood F.
Myosoton aquaticum	Water Chickweed
Myosurus minimus	Mousetail
Myrica gale	Bog Myrtle
Myriophyllum alterniflorum	Alternate Water-milfoil
spicatum	Spiked W.
verticillatum	Whorled W.
Myrrhis odorata	Sweet Cicely
Najas flexilis	Slender Naiad
marina	Holly-leaved N.
Narcissus × biflorus *see*	
N. × medioluteus	
hispanicus	Spanish Daffodil
medioluteus	Primrose-peerless
obvallaris	Tenby Daffodil
pseudonarcissus	Wild D.
Nardurus maritimus	Mat-grass Fescue
Nardus stricta	Mat-grass
Narthecium ossifragum	Bog Asphodel

Naumburgia thyrsiflora *see*
   Lysimachia t.

Neotinea intacta   Dense-flowered Orchid

Neottia nidus-avis   Bird's-nest Orchid

Nepeta cataria   Cat-mint

Nuphar lutea   Yellow Water-lily
   pumila   Least W.

Nymphaea alba   White Water-lily

Nymphoides peltata   Fringed Water-lily

Odontites verna   Red Bartsia

Oenanthe aquatica   Fine-leaved Water-dropwort
   crocata   Hemlock W.
   fistulosa   Tubular W.
   fluviatilis   River W.
   lachenalii   Parsley W.
   pimpinelloides   Corky-fruited W.
   silaifolia   Narrow-leaved W.

Oenothera biennis   Common Evening-primrose
   erythrosepala   Large-flowered E.
   parviflora   Small-flowered E.
   stricta   Fragrant E.

Omphalodes verna   Blue-eyed-Mary

Onobrychis viciifolia   Sainfoin

Ononis reclinata   Small Restharrow
   repens   Common R.
   spinosa   Spiny R.

Onopordon acanthium   Cotton Thistle

Ophioglossum vulgatum Adder's-tongue

Ophrys apifera   Bee Orchid
   fuciflora   Late Spider-orchid
   insectifera   Fly Orchid
   sphegodes   Early Spider-orchid

Orchis laxiflora	Loose-flowered Orchid
mascula	Early-purple O.
militaris	Military O.
morio	Green-winged O.
purpurea	Lady O.
simia	Monkey O.
ustulata	Burnt O.
Origanum vulgare	Marjoram
Ornithogalum nutans	Drooping Star-of-Bethlehem
pyrenaicum	Spiked S.
umbellatum	Star-of-Bethlehem
Ornithopus perpusillus	Bird's-foot
pinnatus	Orange B.
Orobanche alba	Thyme Broomrape
caryophyllacea	Bedstraw B.
elatior	Knapweed B.
hederae	Ivy B.
maritima	Carrot B.
minor	Common B.
picridis	Oxtongue B.
purpurea	Yarrow B.
ramosa	Hemp B.
rapum-genistae	Greater B.
reticulata	Thistle B.
Orthilia secunda	Serrated Wintergreen
Osmunda regalis	Royal Fern
Otanthus maritimus	Cottonweed
Oxalis acetosella	Wood-sorrel
Oxyria digyna	Mountain Sorrel
Oxytropis campestris	Yellow Oxytropis
halleri	Purple O.
Paeonia mascula	Peony
Papaver argemone	Prickly Poppy
dubium	Long-headed P.
hybridum	Rough P.
lecoqii	Yellow-juiced P.

Papaver—*continued*
  rhoeas — Common Poppy
  somniferum — Opium P.

Parapholis incurva — Curved Hard-grass
  strigosa — Hard-grass

Parentucellia viscosa — Yellow Bartsia

Parietaria diffusa *see*
    P.judaica
  judaica — Pellitory-of-the-wall

Paris quadrifolia — Herb-Paris

Parnassia palustris — Grass-of-Parnassus

Pastinaca sativa — Wild Parsnip

Pedicularis palustris — Marsh Lousewort
  sylvatica — Lousewort

Pentaglottis sempervirens — Green Alkanet

Peplis portula — Water-purslane

Pernettya mucronata — Prickly Heath

Petasites albus — White Butterbur
  fragrans — Winter Heliotrope
  hybridus — Butterbur
  japonicus — Giant B.

Petrorhagia nanteuilii — Childling Pink

Petroselinum crispum — Garden Parsley
  segetum — Corn P.

Peucedanum officinale — Hog's Fennel
  ostruthium — Masterwort
  palustre — Milk-parsley

Phalaris arundinacea — Reed Canary-grass
  canariensis — Canary-grass
  minor — Lesser C.

Phleum alpinum — Alpine Cat's-tail
  arenarium — Sand C.
  bertolonii — Smaller C.

Phleum phleoides

Phleum—*continued*
  phleoides   Purple-stem Cat's-tail
  pratense   Timothy

Phragmites australis   Common Reed
  communis *see* P.australis

Phyllitis scolopendrium   Hart's-tongue

Phyllodoce caerulea   Blue Heath

Physalis alkekengi   Cape-gooseberry

Physospermum cornubiense Bladderseed

Phyteuma spicatum   Spiked Rampion
  tenerum   Round-headed R.

Picea abies   Norway Spruce
  sitchensis   Sitka S.

Picris echioides   Bristly Oxtongue
  hieracioides   Hawkweed O.

Pilosella *see* Hieracium

Pilularia globulifera   Pillwort

Pimpinella major   Greater Burnet-saxifrage
  saxifraga   Burnet-saxifrage

Pinguicula grandiflora   Large-flowered Butterwort
  lusitanica   Pale B.
  vulgaris   Common B.

Pinus pinaster   Maritime Pine
  sylvestris   Scots P.

Plantago coronopus   Buck's-horn Plantain
  lanceolata   Ribwort P.
  major   Greater P.
  maritima   Sea P.
  media   Hoary P.

Platanthera bifolia   Lesser Butterfly-orchid
  chlorantha   Greater B.

Platanus × hybrida   London Plane

Poa alpina	Alpine Meadow-grass
angustifolia	Narrow-leaved M.
annua	Annual M.
bulbosa	Bulbous M.
chaixii	Broad-leaved M.
compressus	Flattened M.
flexuosa	Wavy M.
glauca	Glaucous M.
infirma	Early M.
nemoralis	Wood M.
palustris	Swamp M.
pratensis	Smooth M.
pratensis subsp.	
angustifolia *see*	
P.angustifolia	
subcaerulea	Spreading M.
trivialis	Rough M.
Polemonium caeruleum	Jacob's-ladder
Polycarpon tetraphyllum	Four-leaved Allseed
Polygala amara	Dwarf Milkwort
calcarea	Chalk M.
serpyllifolia	Heath M.
vulgaris	Common M.
Polygonatum multiflorum	Solomon's-seal
odoratum	Angular S.
verticillatum	Whorled S.
Polygonum amphibium	Amphibious Bistort
amplexicaule	Red B.
aubertii	Russian-vine
aviculare	Knotgrass
baldschuanicum *see*	
P.aubertii	
bistorta	Common Bistort
campanulatum	Lesser Knotweed
convolvulus	Black-bindweed
cuspidatum	Japanese Knotweed
dumetorum	Copse-bindweed
hydropiper	Water-pepper
lapathifolium	Pale Persicaria
maritimum	Sea Knotgrass
minus	Small Water-pepper
mite	Tasteless W.
persicaria	Redshank
polystachyum	Himalayan Knotweed

Polygonum—*continued*
raii	Ray's Knotgrass
sachalinense	Giant Knotweed
viviparum	Alpine Bistort

Polypodium vulgare	Polypody

Polypogon monspeliensis	Annual Beard-grass

Polystichum aculeatum	Hard Shield-fern
lonchitis	Holly Fern
setiferum	Soft Shield-fern

Populus alba	White Poplar
× canadensis	Italian P.
canescens	Grey P.
gileadensis	Balsam P.
nigra	Black P.
tremula	Aspen

Potamogeton acutifolius	Sharp-leaved Pondweed
alpinus	Red P.
berchtoldii	Small P.
coloratus	Fen P.
compressus	Grass-wrack P.
crispus	Curled P.
epihydrus	American P.
filiformis	Slender-leaved P.
friesii	Flat-stalked P.
gramineus	Various-leaved P.
lucens	Shining P.
natans	Broad-leaved P.
nodosus	Loddon P.
obtusifolius	Blunt-leaved P.
pectinatus	Fennel P.
perfoliatus	Perfoliate P.
polygonifolius	Bog P.
praelongus	Long-stalked P.
pusillus	Lesser P.
rutilus	Shetland P.
trichoides	Hairlike P.

Potentilla anglica	Trailing Tormentil
anserina	Silverweed
argentea	Hoary Cinquefoil
crantzii	Alpine C.
erecta	Tormentil
fruticosa	Shrubby Cinquefoil
norvegica	Ternate-leaved C.

Potentilla—*continued*
  palustris   Marsh Cinquefoil
  recta   Sulphur C.
  reptans   Creeping C.
  rupestris   Rock C. .
  sterilis   Barren Strawberry
  tabernaemontani   Spring Cinquefoil

Poterium polygamum   Fodder Burnet
  sanguisorba   Salad B.

Primula elatior   Oxlip
  farinosa   Bird's-eye Primrose
  scotica   Scottish P.
  veris   Cowslip
  vulgaris   Primrose

Prunella laciniata   Cut-leaved Selfheal
  vulgaris   Selfheal

Prunus avium   Wild Cherry
  cerasifera   Cherry Plum
  cerasus   Dwarf Cherry
  domestica   Wild Plum
  laurocerasus   Cherry Laurel
  lusitanica   Portugal L.
  padus   Bird Cherry
  spinosa   Blackthorn

Pseudorchis albida   Small-white Orchid

Pseudotsuga menziesii   Douglas Fir

Pteridium aquilinum   Bracken

Puccinellia capillaris   Northern Saltmarsh-grass
  distans   Reflexed S.
  fasciculata   Borrer's S.
  maritima   Common S.
  pseudodistans   Greater S.
  rupestris   Stiff S.

Pulicaria dysenterica   Common Fleabane
  vulgaris   Small F.

Pulmonaria longifolia   Narrow-leaved Lungwort
  officinalis   Lungwort

Pulsatilla vulgaris   Pasqueflower

Pyrola media	Intermediate Wintergreen
minor	Common W.
rotundifolia	Round-leaved W.
Pyrus communis	Wild Pear
Quercus cerris	Turkey Oak
ilex	Evergreen O.
petraea	Sessile O.
robur	Pedunculate O.
Radiola linoides	Allseed
Ranunculus acris	Meadow Buttercup
aquatilis	Common Water-crowfoot
arvensis	Corn Buttercup
auricomus	Goldilocks B.
baudotii	Brackish Water-crowfoot
bulbosus	Bulbous Buttercup
circinatus	Fan-leaved Water-crowfoot
ficaria	Lesser Celandine
flammula	Lesser Spearwort
fluitans	River Water-crowfoot
hederaceus	Ivy-leaved Crowfoot
lenormandii *see*	
R.omiophyllus	
lingua	Greater Spearwort
marginatus	St. Martin's Buttercup
omiophyllus	Round-leaved Crowfoot
ophioglossifolius	Adder's-tongue Spearwort
paludosus	Jersey Buttercup
parviflorus	Small-flowered B.
repens	Creeping B.
reptans	Creeping Spearwort
sardous	Hairy Buttercup
sceleratus	Celery-leaved B.
trichophyllus	Thread-leaved Water-crowfoot
tripartitus	Three-lobed Crowfoot
Raphanus maritimus	Sea Radish
raphanistrum	Wild R.
sativus	Garden R.
Rapistrum perenne	Steppe Cabbage
rugosum	Bastard C.

Reseda alba	White Mignonette
lutea	Wild M.
luteola	Weld
Rhamnus catharticus	Buckthorn
Rhinanthus minor	Yellow Rattle
Rhododendron ponticum	Rhododendron
Rhynchosinapis cheiranthos	Wallflower Cabbage
monensis	Isle of Man C.
wrightii	Lundy C.
Rhynchospora alba	White Beak-sedge
fusca	Brown B.
Ribes alpinum	Mountain Currant
nigrum	Black C.
rubrum	Red C.
sanguineum	Flowering C.
spicatum	Downy C.
sylvestre *see* R.rubrum	
uva-crispa	Gooseberry
Robinia pseudoacacia	Acacia
Roemeria hybrida	Violet Horned-poppy
Romulea columnae	Sand Crocus
Rorippa amphibia	Great Yellow-cress
austriaca	Austrian Y.
islandica	Marsh Y.
nasturtium-aquaticum	Water-cress
sylvestris	Creeping Yellow-cress
Rosa arvensis	Field Rose
canina	Dog R.
pimpinellifolia	Burnet R.
rubiginosa	Sweet Briar
rugosa	Japanese Rose
tomentosa	Downy R.
Rubia peregrina	Wild Madder
Rubus caesius	Dewberry
chamaemorus	Cloudberry
fruticosus	Bramble

Rubus—*continued*
idaeus	Raspberry
saxatilis	Stone Bramble

Rumex acetosa	Common Sorrel
acetosella	Sheep's Sorrel
alpinus	Monk's-rhubarb
aquaticus	Scottish Dock
conglomeratus	Clustered D.
crispus	Curled D.
cristatus	Greek D.
hydrolapathum	Water D.
maritimus	Golden D.
longifolius	Northern D.
obtusifolius	Broad-leaved D.
palustris	Marsh D.
patientia	Patience D.
pulcher	Fiddle D.
rupestris	Shore D.
sanguineus	Wood D.
scutatus	French Sorrel
triangulivalvis	Willow-leaved Dock

Ruppia cirrhosa	Spiral Tasselweed
maritima	Beaked T.
spiralis *see* **R**.cirrhosa	

Ruscus aculeatus	Butcher's-broom

Sagina apetala	Annual Pearlwort
intermedia	Snow P.
maritima	Sea P.
nodosa	Knotted P.
normaniana	Scottish P.
procumbens	Procumbent P.
saginoides	Alpine P.
subulata	Heath P.

Sagittaria rigida	Canadian Arrowhead
sagittifolia	Arrowhead

Salicornia europaea	Glasswort
perennis	Perennial G.

Salix alba	White Willow
arbuscula	Mountain W.
aurita	Eared W.
caprea	Goat W.

Salix—*continued*
cinerea	Grey Willow
fragilis	Crack W.
herbacea	Dwarf W.
lanata	Woolly W.
lapponum	Downy W.
myrsinites	Whortle-leaved W.
nigricans	Dark-leaved W.
pentandra	Bay W.
phylicifolia	Tea-leaved W.
purpurea	Purple W.
repens	Creeping W.
reticulata	Net-leaved W.
triandra	Almond W.
viminalis	Osier
Salsola kali	Prickly Saltwort
pestifer	Spineless S.
Salvia horminoides	Wild Clary
pratensis	Meadow C.
verbenaca	Guernsey C.
verticillata	Whorled C.
Sambucus ebulus	Dwarf Elder
nigra	Elder
racemosa	Red-berried E.
Samolus valerandi	Brookweed
Sanguisorba officinalis	Great Burnet
Sanicula europaea	Sanicle
Saponaria officinalis	Soapwort
Sarothamnus scoparius	Broom
Sarracenia purpurea	Pitcherplant
Satureja montana	Winter Savory
Saussurea alpina	Alpine Saw-wort
Saxifraga aizoides	Yellow Saxifrage
cernua	Drooping S.
cespitosa	Tufted S.
granulata	Meadow S.
hirculus	Marsh S.

Saxifraga—*continued*
  hirsuta   Kidney S.
  hypnoides   Mossy S.
  nivalis   Alpine S.
  oppositifolia   Purple S.
  rivularis   Highland S.
  rosacea   Irish S.
  spathularis   St. Patrick's-cabbage
  stellaris   Starry Saxifrage
  tridactylites   Rue-leaved S.
  umbrosa   Londonpride

Scabiosa columbaria   Small Scabious

Scandix pecten-veneris   Shepherd's-needle

Scheuchzeria palustris   Rannoch-rush

Schoenoplectus *see* Scirpus

Schoenus ferrugineus   Brown Bog-rush
  nigricans   Black B.

Scilla autumnalis   Autumn Squill
  verna   Spring S.

Scirpus americanus   Sharp Club-rush
  cernuus   Slender C.
  cespitosus   Deergrass
  fluitans   Floating Club-rush
  holoschoenus   Round-headed C.
  lacustris   Common C.
  maritimus   Sea C.
  setaceus   Bristle C.
  sylvaticus   Wood C.
  tabernaemontani   Grey C.
  triquetrus   Triangular C.

Scleranthus annuus   Annual Knawel
  perennis   Perennial K.

Scorzonera humilis   Viper's-grass

Scrophularia aquatica *see*
     S.auriculata
  auriculata   Water Figwort
  nodosa   Common F.
  scorodonia   Balm-leaved F.
  umbrosa   Green F.
  vernalis   Yellow F.

Scutellaria galericulata	Skullcap
minor	Lesser S.
Sedum acre	Biting Stonecrop
album	White S.
anglicum	English S.
dasyphyllum	Thick-leaved S.
forsteranum	Rock S.
reflexum	Reflexed S.
rosea	Roseroot
sexangulare	Tasteless Stonecrop
telephium	Orpine
villosum	Hairy Stonecrop
Selaginella selaginoides	Lesser Clubmoss
Selinum carvifolia	Cambridge Milk-parsley
Sempervivum tectorum	House-leek
Senecio aquaticus	Marsh Ragwort
cineraria	Silver R.
erucifolius	Hoary R.
fluviatilis	Broad-leaved R.
integrifolius	Field Fleawort
jacobaea	Common Ragwort
paludosus	Fen R.
palustris	Marsh Fleawort
smithii	Magellan Ragwort
squalidus	Oxford R.
sylvaticus	Heath Groundsel
viscosus	Sticky G.
vulgaris	Groundsel
Serratula tinctoria	Saw-wort
Seseli libanotis	Moon Carrot
Sesleria albicans *see*	
S.caerulea	
caerulea	Blue Moor-grass
Setaria lutescens	Yellow Bristle-grass
verticillata	Rough B.
viridis	Green B.
Sherardia arvensis	Field Madder
Sibbaldia procumbens	Sibbaldia

Sibthorpia europaea	Cornish Moneywort
Sieglingia decumbens	Heath-grass
Silaum silaus	Pepper-saxifrage
Silene acaulis	Moss Campion
alba	White Campion
armeria	Sweet-William Catchfly
conica	Sand Catchfly
dichotoma	Forked Catchfly
dioica	Red Campion
gallica	Small-flowered Catchfly
italica	Italian Catchfly
maritima	Sea Campion
noctiflora	Night-flowering Catchfly
nutans	Nottingham Catchfly
otites	Spanish Catchfly
vulgaris	Bladder Campion
Silybum marianum	Milk Thistle
Simethis planifolia	Kerry Lily
Sinapis alba	White Mustard
arvensis	Charlock
Sison amomum	Stone Parsley
Sisymbrium altissimum	Tall Rocket
irio	London-rocket
loeselii	False L.
officinale	Hedge Mustard
orientale	Eastern Rocket
Sisyrinchium bermudiana	Blue-eyed-grass
californicum	Yellow-eyed-grass
Sium latifolium	Greater Water-parsnip
Smyrnium olusatrum	Alexanders
Solanum dulcamara	Bittersweet
nigrum	Black Nightshade
sarrachoides	Green N.
Soleirolia soleirolii	Mind-your-own-business
Solidago canadensis	Canadian Goldenrod
virgaurea	Goldenrod

Sonchus arvensis	Perennial Sow-thistle
asper	Prickly S.
oleraceus	Smooth S.
palustris	Marsh S.
Sorbus aria	Common Whitebeam
aucuparia	Rowan
domestica	Service-tree
intermedia	Swedish Whitebeam
latifolia	Broad-leaved W.
torminalis	Wild Service-tree
Sparganium angustifolium	Floating Bur-reed
emersum	Unbranched B.
erectum	Branched B.
minimum	Least B.
Spartina alterniflora	Smooth Cord-grass
anglica	Common C.
maritima	Small C.
townsendii	Townsend's C.
Spartium junceum	Spanish Broom
Spergula arvensis	Corn Spurrey
Spergularia marina	Lesser Sea-spurrey
media	Greater S.
rubra	Sand Spurrey
rupicola	Rock Sea-spurrey
Spiraea salicifolia	Bridewort
Spiranthes aestivalis	Summer Lady's-tresses
romanzoffiana	Irish L.
spiralis	Autumn L.
Stachys alpina	Limestone Woundwort
arvensis	Field W.
germanica	Downy W.
palustris	Marsh W.
sylvatica	Hedge W.
Stellaria alsine	Bog Stitchwort
graminea	Lesser S.
holostea	Greater S.
media	Common Chickweed
neglecta	Greater C.
nemorum	Wood Stitchwort

Stellaria—*continued*
   pallida   Lesser Chickweed
   palustris   Marsh Stitchwort

Stratiotes aloides   Water-soldier

Suaeda fruticosa *see* S.vera
   maritima   Annual Sea-blite
   vera   Shrubby S.

Subularia aquatica   Awlwort

Succisa pratensis   Devil's-bit Scabious

Swida sanguinea   Dogwood

Symphoricarpos rivularis   Snowberry

Symphytum asperum   Rough Comfrey
   grandiflorum   Creeping C.
   officinale   Common C.
   orientale   White C.
   tuberosum   Tuberous C.
   × uplandicum   Russian C.

Syringa vulgaris   Lilac

Tamarix anglica   Tamarisk

Tamus communis   Black Bryony

Tanacetum parthenium   Feverfew
   vulgare   Tansy

Taraxacum officinale   Dandelion

Taxus baccata   Yew

Teesdalia nudicaulis   Shepherd's Cress

Tetragonolobus maritimus   Dragon's-teeth

Teucrium botrys   Cut-leaved Germander
   chamaedrys   Wall G.
   scordium   Water G.
   scorodonia   Wood Sage

Thalictrum alpinum   Alpine Meadow-rue
   flavum   Common M.
   minus   Lesser M.

Thelycrania sanguinea *see*
   Swida s.

Thelypteris dryopteris *see*
   Gymnocarpium d.
   limbosperma   Lemon-scented Fern
   oreopteris *see*
      T.limbosperma
   palustris   Marsh F.
   phegopteris   Beech F.

Thesium humifusum   Bastard-toadflax

Thlaspi alliaceum   Garlic Penny-cress
   alpestre   Alpine P.
   arvense   Field P.
   perfoliatum   Perfoliate P.

Thymus drucei   Wild Thyme
   pulegioides   Large T.
   serpyllum   Breckland T.

Tilia cordata   Small-leaved Lime
   × europaea *see* T. × vulgaris
   platyphyllos   Large-leaved L.
   × vulgaris   Lime

Tofieldia pusilla   Scottish Asphodel

Tolmiea menziesii   Pick-a-back-plant

Tordylium maximum   Hartwort

Torilis arvensis   Spreading Hedge-parsley
   japonica   Upright H.
   nodosa   Knotted H.

Trachystemon orientalis   Abraham-Isaac-Jacob

Tragopogon porrifolius   Salsify
   pratensis   Goat's-beard

Trichomanes speciosum   Killarney Fern

Trichophorum cespitosum
   see Scirpus cespitosus

Trientalis europaea	Chickweed Wintergreen
Trifolium arvense	Hare's-foot Clover
bocconei	Twin-flowered C.
campestre	Hop Trefoil
dubium	Lesser T.
fragiferum	Strawberry Clover
glomeratum	Clustered C.
hybridum	Alsike C.
incarnatum	Crimson C.
medium	Zigzag C.
micranthum	Slender Trefoil
molinerii	Long-headed Clover
ochroleucon	Sulphur C.
ornithopodioides	Fenugreek
pratense	Red Clover
repens	White C.
resupinatum	Reversed C.
scabrum	Rough C.
squamosum	Sea C.
stellatum	Starry C.
striatum	Knotted C.
strictum	Upright C.
subterraneum	Subterranean C.
suffocatum	Suffocated C.
Triglochin maritima	Sea Arrowgrass
palustris	Marsh A.
Trinia glauca	Honewort
Tripleurospermum maritimum subsp. inodorum	Scentless Mayweed
Trisetum flavescens	Yellow Oat-grass
Trollius europaeus	Globeflower
Tuberaria guttata	Spotted Rock-rose
Tulipa sylvestris	Wild Tulip
Turritis glabra	Tower Mustard
Tussilago farfara	Colt's-foot
Typha angustifolia	Lesser Bulrush
latifolia	Bulrush

Ulex europaeus	Gorse
gallii	Western G.
minor	Dwarf G.
Ulmus carpinifolia	Small-leaved Elm
glabra	Wych E.
procera	English E.
Umbilicus rupestris	Navelwort
Urtica dioica	Common Nettle
pilulifera	Roman N.
urens	Small N.
Utricularia intermedia	Intermediate Bladderwort
minor	Lesser B.
vulgaris	Greater B.
Vaccaria pyramidata	Cowherb
Vaccinium macrocarpon	American Cranberry
microcarpum	Small C.
myrtillus	Bilberry
oxycoccos	Cranberry
uliginosum	Bog Bilberry
vitis-idaea	Cowberry
Valeriana dioica	Marsh Valerian
officinalis	Common V.
pyrenaica	Pyrenean V.
Valerianella carinata	Keeled-fruited Cornsalad
dentata	Narrow-fruited C.
eriocarpa	Hairy-fruited C.
locusta	Common C.
rimosa	Broad-fruited C.
Verbascum blattaria	Moth Mullein
lychnitis	White M.
nigrum	Dark M.
phlomoides	Orange M.
pulverulentum	Hoary M.
thapsus	Great M.
virgatum	Twiggy M.
Verbena officinalis	Vervain

61

Veronica agrestis	Green Field-speedwell
alpina	Alpine Speedwell
anagallis-aquatica	Blue Water-speedwell
arvensis	Wall Speedwell
beccabunga	Brooklime
catenata	Pink Water-speedwell
chamaedrys	Germander Speedwell
filiformis	Slender S.
fruticans	Rock S.
hederifolia	Ivy-leaved S.
montana	Wood S.
officinalis	Heath S.
peregrina	American S.
persica	Common Field-speedwell
polita	Grey F.
praecox	Breckland Speedwell
scutellata	Marsh S.
serpyllifolia	Thyme-leaved S.
spicata	Spiked S.
triphyllos	Fingered S.
verna	Spring S.
Viburnum lantana	Wayfaring-tree
opulus	Guelder-rose
tinus	Laurustinus
Vicia angustifolia	Narrow-leaved Vetch
bithynica	Bithynian V.
cracca	Tufted V.
hirsuta	Hairy Tare
hybrida	Hairy Yellow-vetch
lathyroides	Spring Vetch
lutea	Yellow-vetch
orobus	Wood Bitter-vetch
sativa	Common Vetch
sepium	Bush V.
sylvatica	Wood V.
tenuifolia	Fine-leaved V.
tenuissima	Slender Tare
tetrasperma	Smooth T.
villosa	Fodder Vetch
Vinca major	Greater Periwinkle
minor	Lesser P.
Viola arvensis	Field Pansy
canina	Heath Dog-violet
hirta	Hairy Violet
kitaibeliana	Dwarf Pansy

Viola—*continued*
   lactea   Pale Dog-violet
   lutea   Mountain Pansy
   odorata   Sweet Violet
   palustris   Marsh V.
   persicifolia   Fen V.
   reichenbachiana   Early Dog-violet
   riviniana   Common D.
   rupestris   Teesdale Violet
   stagnina *see* V.persicifolia
   tricolor   Wild Pansy

Viscum album   Mistletoe

Vitis vinifera   Grape-vine

Vulpia ambigua   Bearded Fescue
   bromoides   Squirreltail F.
   megalura   Foxtail F.
   membranacea   Dune F.
   myuros   Rat's-tail F.

Wahlenbergia hederacea   Ivy-leaved Bellflower

Wolffia arrhiza   Rootless Duckweed

Woodsia alpina   Alpine Woodsia
   ilvensis   Oblong W.

Xanthium spinosum   Spiny Cocklebur
   strumarium   Rough C.

Zannichellia palustris   Horned Pondweed

Zerna *see* Bromus

Zostera angustifolia   Narrow-leaved Eelgrass
   marina   Eelgrass
   noltii   Dwarf E.

English–Latin

Abraham-Isaac-Jacob	Trachystemon orientalis
Acacia	Robinia pseudoacacia
Aconite, Winter	Eranthis hyemalis
Adder's-tongue	Ophioglossum vulgatum
Agrimony *see also* Hemp-a.	

Agrimony
  Fragrant
	Agrimonia eupatoria
	  procera Wallr.

Alder
  Grey
	Alnus glutinosa
	  incana

Alexanders	Smyrnium olusatrum

Alison, Hoary
  Small
  Sweet
	Berteroa incana
	  Alyssum alyssoides
	  Lobularia maritima

Alkanet
  Green
	Anchusa officinalis
	  Pentaglottis sempervirens

Allseed
  Four-leaved
	Radiola linoides
	  Polycarpon tetraphyllum

Alpine-sedge, Black
  Close-headed
  Scorched
	Carex atrata
	  norvegica
	  atrofusca

Amaranth, Common
  Green
	Amaranthus retroflexus
	  hybridus

Anemone, Blue
  Wood
  Yellow
	Anemone apennina
	  nemorosa
	  ranunculoides

Angelica, Garden	Angelica archangelica
Wild	sylvestris
Apple *see also* Thorn-a.	
Apple, Crab	Malus sylvestris
Arabis, Garden	Arabis caucasica
Archangel, Yellow	Lamiastrum galeobdolon (L.) Ehrend. & Polatsch.
Arrowgrass, Marsh	Triglochin palustris
Sea	maritima
Arrowhead	Sagittaria sagittifolia
Canadian	rigida
Asarabacca	Asarum europaeum
Ash	Fraxinus excelsior
Asparagus, Wild	Asparagus officinalis
Aspen	Populus tremula
Asphodel, Bog	Narthecium ossifragum
Scottish	Tofieldia pusilla
Aster, Goldilocks	Crinitaria linosyris
Sea	Aster tripolium
Astrantia	Astrantia major
Avens, Mountain	Dryas octopetala
Water	Geum rivale
Wood	urbanum
Awlwort	Subularia aquatica
Azalea, Trailing	Loiseleuria procumbens
Balm	Melissa officinalis
Bastard	Melittis melissophyllum
Balsam, Indian	Impatiens glandulifera
Orange	capensis
Small	parviflora
Touch-me-not	noli-tangere

Baneberry	Actaea spicata
Barberry	Berberis vulgaris
Barley, Foxtail	Hordeum jubatum
Meadow	secalinum
Sea	marinum
Wall	murinum
Wood	Hordelymus europaeus
Bartsia, Alpine	Bartsia alpina
Red	Odontites verna
Yellow	Parentucellia viscosa
Basil, Wild	Clinopodium vulgare
Bastard-toadflax	Thesium humifusum
Beak-sedge, Brown	Rhynchospora fusca
White	alba
Beam *see* Hornbeam, Whitebeam	
Bearberry	Arctostaphylos uva-ursi
Alpine	Arctous alpinus
Beard-grass, Annual	Polypogon monspeliensis
Bear's-breech	Acanthus mollis
Bedstraw *see also* Marsh-b.	
Bedstraw, Fen	Galium uliginosum
Heath	saxatile
Hedge	mollugo
Lady's	verum
Limestone	sterneri
Northern	boreale
Slender	pumilum
Wall	parisiense
Beech	Fagus sylvatica
Beet, Sea	Beta vulgaris subsp. maritima
Beggarticks	Bidens frondosa
Bellflower, Clustered	Campanula glomerata
Creeping	rapunculoides

Bellflower—*continued*
Giant	Campanula latifolia
Ivy-leaved	Wahlenbergia hederacea
Nettle-leaved	Campanula trachelium
Peach-leaved	persicifolia
Rampion	rapunculus
Spreading	patula

Bent *see also* Silky-b.

Bent, Black	Agrostis gigantea
Bristle	setacea
Brown	canina
Common	tenuis
Creeping	stolonifera
Water	semiverticillata

Bermuda-grass	Cynodon dactylon

Betony	Betonica officinalis

Bilberry	Vaccinium myrtillus
Bog	uliginosum

Bindweed *see also* Black-b.,
    Copse-b.

Bindweed, Field	Convolvulus arvensis
Hairy	Calystegia pulchra Brummitt & Heywood
Hedge	sepium
Large	sylvatica
Sea	soldanella

Birch, Downy	Betula pubescens
Dwarf	nana
Silver	pendula

Bird's-foot	Ornithopus perpusillus
Orange	pinnatus

Bird's-foot-trefoil, Common	Lotus corniculatus
Greater	uliginosus
Hairy	subuliflorus Lag.
Narrow-leaved	tenuis
Slender	angustissimus

Bird's-nest, Yellow	Monotropa hypopitys

Birthwort	Aristolochia clematitis

Bistort, Alpine	Polygonum viviparum
Amphibious	amphibium
Common	bistorta
Red	amplexicaule
Bitter-cress, Hairy	Cardamine hirsuta
Large	amara
Narrow-leaved	impatiens
Wavy	flexuosa
Bittersweet	Solanum dulcamara
Bitter-vetch, Wood	Vicia orobus
Black-bindweed	Polygonum convolvulus
Black-grass	Alopecurus myosuroides
Blackthorn	Prunus spinosa
Bladder-fern, Brittle	Cystopteris fragilis
Mountain	montana
Bladder-sedge	Carex vesicaria
Mountain	stenolepis
Bladderseed	Physospermum cornubiense
Bladder-senna	Colutea arborescens
Bladderwort, Greater	Utricularia vulgaris
Intermediate	intermedia
Lesser	minor
Blinks	Montia fontana
Blite *see* Sea-b., Strawberry-b.	
Blood-drop-emlets	Mimulus luteus
Bluebell	Endymion non-scriptus
Spanish	hispanicus
Blue-eyed-grass	Sisyrinchium bermudiana
Blue-eyed-Mary	Omphalodes verna
Bogbean	Menyanthes trifoliata

Bog-rush, Black	Schoenus nigricans
Brown	ferrugineus
Bog-sedge	Carex limosa
Mountain	rariflora
Tall	paupercula
Borage	Borago officinalis
Box	Buxus sempervirens
Bracken	Pteridium aquilinum
Bramble	Rubus fruticosus*
Stone	saxatilis
Briar, Sweet	Rosa rubiginosa†
Bridewort	Spiraea salicifolia
Bristle-grass, Green	Setaria viridis
Rough	verticillata
Yellow	lutescens

Brome *see also* Hairy-b.,
    Soft-b.

Brome, Barren	Bromus sterilis
California	carinatus
Compact	madritensis
Drooping	tectorum
False	Brachypodium sylvaticum
Field	Bromus arvensis
Great	diandrus
Hungarian	inermis
Interrupted	interruptus
Meadow	commutatus
Rescue	willdenowii Kunth
Rye	secalinus
Smooth	racemosus
Upright	erectus
Brooklime	Veronica beccabunga

* There are numerous microspecies which, if correctly identified, should be so indicated.
† The English name may also be applied to *R.micrantha, R.elliptica* and *R.agrestis.* If a correct identification has been made this should be so indicated.

Brookweed	Samolus valerandi

Broom *see also* Butcher's-b.

Broom	Sarothamnus scoparius
Spanish	Spartium junceum

Broomrape, Bedstraw	Orobanche caryophyllacea
Carrot	maritima
Common	minor
Greater	rapum-genistae
Hemp	ramosa
Ivy	hederae
Knapweed	elatior
Oxtongue	picridis
Thistle	reticulata
Thyme	alba
Yarrow	purpurea

Bryony, Black	Tamus communis
White	Bryonia dioica

Buckler-fern, Broad	Dryopteris dilatata
Crested	cristata
Hay-scented	aemula
Narrow	carthusiana (Vill.) H. P. Fuchs
Rigid	villarii

Buckthorn *see also* Sea-b.

Buckthorn	Rhamnus catharticus
Alder	Frangula alnus

Buckwheat	Fagopyrum esculentum

Bugle	Ajuga reptans
Pyramidal	pyramidalis

Bugloss *see also* Viper's-b.

Bugloss	Lycopsis arvensis

Bullwort	Ammi majus

Bulrush	Typha latifolia
Lesser	angustifolia

Burdock, Greater	Arctium lappa
Lesser	minus*
Bur-marigold, Nodding	Bidens cernua
Trifid	tripartita
Burnet, Fodder	Poterium polygamum
Great	Sanguisorba officinalis
Salad	Poterium sanguisorba
Burnet-saxifrage	Pimpinella saxifraga
Greater	major
Bur-parsley, Greater	Caucalis latifolia
Small	platycarpos
Bur-reed, Branched	Sparganium erectum
Floating	angustifolium
Least	minimum
Unbranched	emersum
Butcher's-broom	Ruscus aculeatus
Butterbur	Petasites hybridus
Giant	japonicus
White	albus
Buttercup, Bulbous	Ranunculus bulbosus
Celery-leaved	sceleratus
Corn	arvensis
Creeping	repens
Goldilocks	auricomus
Hairy	sardous
Jersey	paludosus
Meadow	acris
St. Martin's	marginatus
Small-flowered	parviflorus
Butterfly-bush	Buddleja davidii
Butterfly-orchid, Greater	Platanthera chlorantha
Lesser	bifolia
Butterwort, Common	Pinguicula vulgaris
Large-flowered	grandiflora
Pale	lusitanica

* There are closely allied species which, if correctly identified, should be so indicated.

Buttonweed   Cotula coronopifolia

Cabbage *see also*
   St. Patrick's-c.

Cabbage, Bastard   Rapistrum rugosum
  Isle of Man   Rhynchosinapis monensis
  Lundy   wrightii
  Steppe   Rapistrum perenne
  Wallflower   Rhynchosinapis cheiranthos
  Warty   Bunias orientalis
  Wild   Brassica oleracea

Calamint, Common   Calamintha ascendens
  Lesser   nepeta
  Wood   sylvatica

Campion, Bladder   Silene vulgaris
  Moss   acaulis
  Red   dioica
  Sea   maritima
  White   alba

Canary-grass   Phalaris canariensis
  Lesser   minor
  Reed   arundinacea

Candytuft, Wild   Iberis amara

Canterbury-bells   Campanula medium

Cape-gooseberry   Physalis alkekengi

Caraway   Carum carvi
  Whorled   verticillatum

Carrot, Moon   Seseli libanotis
  Wild   Daucus carota

Catchfly, Alpine   Lychnis alpina
  Berry   Cucubalus baccifer
  Forked   Silene dichotoma
  Italian   italica
  Night-flowering   noctiflora
  Nottingham   nutans
  Sand   conica
  Small-flowered   gallica
  Spanish   otites

Catchfly—*continued*
Sticky | Lychnis viscaria
Sweet-William | Silene armeria

Cat-mint | Nepeta cataria

Cat's-ear | Hypochoeris radicata
Smooth | glabra
Spotted | maculata

Cat's-tail, Alpine | Phleum alpinum
Purple-stem | phleoides
Sand | arenarium
Smaller | bertolonii

Celandine, Greater | Chelidonium majus
Lesser | Ranunculus ficaria

Celery, Wild | Apium graveolens

Centaury, Broad-leaved | Centaurium latifolium
Common | erythraea
Guernsey | Exaculum pusillum
Lesser | Centaurium pulchellum
Perennial | scilloides
Seaside | littorale
Slender | tenuiflorum
Tufted | capitatum
Yellow | Cicendia filiformis

Chaffweed | Anagallis minima

Chamomile | Chamaemelum nobile
Corn | Anthemis arvensis
Stinking | cotula
Yellow | tinctoria

Charlock | Sinapis arvensis

Cherry, Bird | Prunus padus
Dwarf | cerasus
Wild | avium

Chervil, Bur | Anthriscus caucalis
Garden | A. cerefolium
Golden | Chaerophyllum aureum
Rough | C. temulentum

Chestnut *see also* Horse-c.
Chestnut, Sweet | Castanea sativa

Chickweed, Common	Stellaria media
Greater	neglecta
Lesser	pallida
Upright	Moenchia erecta
Water	Myosoton aquaticum
Chicory	Cichorium intybus
Chives	Allium schoenoprasum
Cicely, Sweet	Myrrhis odorata
Cinquefoil, Alpine	Potentilla crantzii
Creeping	reptans
Hoary	argentea
Marsh	palustris
Rock	rupestris
Shrubby	fruticosa
Spring	tabernaemontani
Sulphur	recta
Ternate-leaved	norvegica
Clary, Guernsey	Salvia verbenaca
Meadow	pratensis
Whorled	verticillata
Wild	horminoides
Cleavers	Galium aparine
Corn	tricornutum
False	spurium
Cloudberry	Rubus chamaemorus
Clover, Alsike	Trifolium hybridum
Clustered	glomeratum
Crimson	incarnatum
Hare's-foot	arvense
Knotted	striatum
Long-headed	molinerii
Red	pratense
Reversed	resupinatum
Rough	scabrum
Sea	squamosum
Starry	stellatum
Strawberry	fragiferum
Subterranean	subterraneum
Suffocated	suffocatum
Sulphur	ochroleucon
Twin-flowered	bocconei

Clover—*continued*
  Upright   Trifolium strictum
  White   repens
  Zigzag   medium

Clubmoss, Alpine   Lycopodium alpinum
  Fir   selago
  Interrupted   annotinum
  Lesser   Selaginella selaginoides
  Marsh   Lycopodium inundatum
  Stag's-horn   clavatum

Club-rush, Bristle   Scirpus setaceus
  Common   lacustris
  Floating   fluitans
  Grey   tabernaemontani
  Round-headed   holoschoenus
  Sea   maritimus
  Sharp   americanus
  Slender   cernuus
  Triangular   triquetrus
  Wood   sylvaticus

Cocklebur, Rough   Xanthium strumarium
  Spiny   spinosum

Cock's-foot   Dactylis glomerata

Cockspur   Echinochloa crus-galli

Colt's-foot   Tussilago farfara
  Purple   Homogyne alpina

Columbine   Aquilegia vulgaris

Comfrey, Common   Symphytum officinale
  Creeping   grandiflorum
  Rough   asperum
  Russian   × uplandicum
  Tuberous   tuberosum
  White   orientale

Copse-bindweed   Polygonum dumetorum

Coral-necklace   Illecebrum verticillatum

Coralroot   Cardamine bulbifera

Cord-grass, Common	Spartina anglica
Small	maritima
Smooth	alterniflora
Townsend's	× townsendii
Coriander	Coriandrum sativum
Corncockle	Agrostemma githago
Cornel, Dwarf	Chamaepericlymenum suecicum
Cornflower	Centaurea cyanus
Perennial	montana
Cornsalad, Broad-fruited	Valerianella rimosa
Common	locusta
Hairy-fruited	eriocarpa
Keeled-fruited	carinata
Narrow-fruited	dentata
Corydalis, Climbing	Corydalis claviculata
Yellow	lutea
Cotoneaster, Himalayan	Cotoneaster simonsii
Small-leaved	microphyllus
Wall	horizontalis
Wild	integerrimus
Cottongrass, Broad-leaved	Eriophorum latifolium
Common	angustifolium
Hare's-tail	vaginatum
Slender	gracile
Cottonweed	Otanthus maritimus
Couch, Bearded	Agropyron caninum
Common	repens
Don's	donianum
Sand	junceiforme
Sea	pungens
Cowbane	Cicuta virosa
Cowberry	Vaccinium vitis-idaea
Cowherb	Vaccaria pyramidata
Cowslip	Primula veris

Cow-wheat, Common	Melampyrum pratense
Crested	cristatum
Field	arvense
Small	sylvaticum
Cranberry	Vaccinium oxycoccos
American	macrocarpon
Small	microcarpum
Crane's-bill, Bloody	Geranium sanguineum
Cut-leaved	dissectum
Dove's-foot	molle
Dusky	phaeum
French	endressii
Hedgerow	pyrenaicum
Knotted	nodosum
Long-stalked	columbinum
Meadow	pratense
Pencilled	versicolor
Round-leaved	rotundifolium
Shining	lucidum
Small-flowered	pusillum
Wood	sylvaticum
Creeping-Jenny	Lysimachia nummularia

Cress *see also* Bitter-c.,
    Penny-c., Rock-c.,
    Swine-c., Water-c.,
    Winter-c., Yellow-c.

Cress, Garden	Lepidium sativum
Hoary	Cardaria draba
Shepherd's	Teesdalia nudicaulis
Thale	Arabidopsis thaliana
Tower	Arabis turrita
Crocus, Autumn	Crocus nudiflorus
Saffron	sativus
Sand	Romulea columnae
Spring	Crocus purpureus
Crosswort	Cruciata laevipes Opiz
Crowberry	Empetrum nigrum
Mountain	hermaphroditum

Crowfoot *see also* Water-c.

Crowfoot, Ivy-leaved	Ranunculus hederaceus
Round-leaved	omiophyllus Ten.
Three-lobed	tripartitus
Cuckooflower	Cardamine pratensis
Cudweed, Broad-leaved	Filago pyramidata L.
Common	vulgaris Lam.
Dwarf	Gnaphalium supinum
Heath	sylvaticum
Highland	norvegicum
Jersey	luteoalbum
Marsh	uliginosum
Narrow-leaved	Filago gallica
Red-tipped	lutescens Jord.
Small	minima
Currant, Black	Ribes nigrum
Downy	spicatum
Flowering	sanguineum
Mountain	alpinum
Red	rubrum L.
Cut-grass	Leersia oryzoides
Cyclamen	Cyclamen hederifolium
Cyphel	Cherleria sedoides
Daffodil, Spanish	Narcissus hispanicus
Tenby	obvallaris
Wild	pseudonarcissus

Daisy *see also* Michaelmas-d.

Daisy	Bellis perennis
Oxeye	Leucanthemum vulgare Lam.
Shasta	maximum (Ramond) DC.
Dame's-violet	Hesperis matronalis
Dandelion	Taraxacum officinale*
Darnel	Lolium temulentum

* Dandelions are now the subject of much study. If a correct identification has been made it should be so indicated.

Dead-nettle, Cut-leaved	Lamium hybridum
Henbit	amplexicaule
Northern	moluccellifolium
Red	purpureum
Spotted	maculatum
White	album
Deergrass	Scirpus cespitosus
Dewberry	Rubus caesius
Diapensia	Diapensia lapponica
Dittander	Lepidium latifolium
Dock, Broad-leaved	Rumex obtusifolius
Clustered	conglomeratus
Curled	crispus
Fiddle	pulcher
Golden	maritimus
Greek	cristatus
Marsh	palustris
Northern	longifolius
Patience	patientia
Scottish	aquaticus
Shore	rupestris
Water	hydrolapathum
Willow-leaved	triangulivalvis
Wood	sanguineus
Dodder	Cuscuta epithymum
Flax	epilinum
Greater	europaea
Dog's-tail, Crested	Cynosurus cristatus
Rough	echinatus
Dog-violet ,Common	Viola riviniana
Early	reichenbachiana
Heath	canina
Pale	lactea
Dogwood	Swida sanguinea Opiz
Dragon's-teeth	Tetragonolobus maritimus
Dropwort *see also* Water-d.	
Dropwort	Filipendula vulgaris

Duckweed, Common	Lemna minor
Fat	gibba
Greater	polyrrhiza
Ivy-leaved	trisulca
Rootless	Wolffia arrhiza
Eelgrass	Zostera marina
Dwarf	noltii
Narrow-leaved	angustifolia

Elder *see also* Ground-e.

Elder	Sambucus nigra
Dwarf	ebulus
Red-berried	racemosa
Elecampane	Inula helenium
Elm, English	Ulmus procera
Small-leaved	carpinifolia*
Wych	glabra
Enchanter's-nightshade	Circaea lutetiana
Alpine	alpina
Upland	intermedia
Eryngo, Field	Eryngium campestre
Evening-primrose, Common	Oenothera biennis
Fragrant	stricta
Large-flowered	erythrosepala
Small-flowered	parviflora
Everlasting, Mountain	Antennaria dioica
Pearly	Anaphalis margaritacea
Everlasting-pea, Broad-	
leaved	Lathyrus latifolius
Narrow-leaved	sylvestris
Eyebright	Euphrasia officinalis†
Irish	salisburgensis

* There are closely allied species which, if correctly identified, should be so indicated.
† There are many microspecies which, if correctly identified, should be so indicated.

Fat-hen	Chenopodium album
Fennel	Foeniculum vulgare
Hog's	Peucedanum officinale
Fen-sedge, Great	Cladium mariscus
Fenugreek	Trifolium ornithopodioides

Fern *see also* Bladder-f.,
    Buckler-f., Filmy-f.,
    Lady-f., Male-f.,
    Shield-f.

Fern, Beech	Thelypteris phegopteris
Hard	Blechnum spicant
Holly	Polystichum lonchitis
Jersey	Anogramma leptophylla
Killarney	Trichomanes speciosum
Lemon-scented	Thelypteris limbosperma (All.) H.P. Fuchs
Limestone	Gymnocarpium robertianum (Hoffm.) Newm.
Maidenhair	Adiantum capillus-veneris
Marsh	Thelypteris palustris
Oak	Gymnocarpium dryopteris (L.) Newm.
Parsley	Cryptogramma crispa
Royal	Osmunda regalis
Water	Azolla filiculoides
Fern-grass	Catapodium rigidum
Sea	marinum

Fescue *see also* Sheep's-f.

Fescue, Bearded	Vulpia ambigua
Blue	Festuca glauca
Dune	Vulpia membranacea
Foxtail	megalura
Giant	Festuca gigantea
Hard	longifolia
Mat-grass	Nardurus maritimus
Meadow	Festuca pratensis
Rat's-tail	Vulpia myuros
Red	Festuca rubra
Rush-leaved	juncifolia
Squirreltail	Vulpia bromoides
Tall	Festuca arundinacea

Fescue—*continued*
  Various-leaved   Festuca heterophylla
  Viviparous   vivipara
  Wood   altissima

Feverfew   Tanacetum parthenium
         (L.) Schultz Bip.

Field-speedwell, Common   Veronica persica
  Green   agrestis
  Grey   polita

Fig *see also* Hottentot-f.

Fig   Ficus carica

Figwort, Balm-leaved   Scrophularia scorodonia
  Common   nodosa
  Green   umbrosa
  Water   auriculata L.
  Yellow   vernalis

Filmy-fern, Tunbridge   Hymenophyllum tunbrigense
  Wilson's   wilsonii

Finger-grass, Hairy   Digitaria sanguinalis
  Smooth   ischaemum

Fir, Douglas   Pseudotsuga menziesii

Flag *see* Sweet-f.

Flat-sedge   Blysmus compressus
  Saltmarsh   rufus

Flax   Linum usitatissimum
  Fairy   catharticum
  Pale   bienne
  Perennial   anglicum

Fleabane, Alpine   Erigeron borealis
  Blue   acer
  Canadian   Conyza canadensis
  Common   Pulicaria dysenterica
  Irish   Inula salicina
  Mexican   Erigeron mucronatus
  Small   Pulicaria vulgaris

Fleawort, Field   Senecio integrifolius
  Marsh   palustris

Flixweed	Descurainia sophia
Flowering-rush	Butomus umbellatus
Fluellen, Round-leaved	Kickxia spuria
Sharp-leaved	elatine
Forget-me-not, Alpine	Myosotis alpestris
Changing	discolor
Creeping	secunda
Early	ramosissima
Field	arvensis
Jersey	sicula
Pale	stolonifera (DC.) Gay ex Leresche & Levier
Tufted	caespitosa
Water	scorpioides
Wood	sylvatica
Foxglove	Digitalis purpurea
Fairy	Erinus alpinus
Fox-sedge, False	Carex otrubae
True	vulpina
Foxtail, Alpine	Alopecurus alpinus
Bulbous	bulbosus
Marsh	geniculatus
Meadow	pratensis
Orange	aequalis
Fritillary	Fritillaria meleagris
Frogbit	Hydrocharis morsus-ranae
Fuchsia	Fuchsia magellanica
Fumitory *see also* Ramping-f.	
Fumitory, Common	Fumaria officinalis
Dense-flowered	densiflora DC.
Few-flowered	vaillantii
Fine-leaved	parviflora
Galingale	Cyperus longus
Brown	fuscus
Garlic, Field	Allium oleraceum
Keeled	carinatum

Gentian, Alpine	Gentiana nivalis
Autumn	Gentianella amarella
Chiltern	germanica
Dune	uliginosa
Early	anglica
Field	campestris
Marsh	Gentiana pneumonanthe
Spring	verna
Germander, Cut-leaved	Teucrium botrys
Wall	chamaedrys
Water	scordium
Gipsywort	Lycopus europaeus
Gladiolus, Wild	Gladiolus illyricus
Glasswort	Salicornia europaea*
Perennial	perennis
Globeflower	Trollius europaeus
Goat's-beard	Tragopogon pratensis
Goat's-rue	Galega officinalis
Goldenrod	Solidago virgaurea
Canadian	canadensis
Golden-saxifrage, Alternate-leaved	Chrysosplenium alternifolium
Opposite-leaved	oppositifolium
Gold-of-pleasure	Camelina sativa
Good-King-Henry	Chenopodium bonus-henricus
Gooseberry *see also* Cape-g.	
Gooseberry	Ribes uva-crispa
Goosefoot, Fig-leaved	Chenopodium ficifolium
Grey	opulifolium
Many-seeded	polyspermum
Maple-leaved	hybridum
Nettle-leaved	murale
Oak-leaved	glaucum

* There are closely allied species which, if correctly identified, should be so indicated

Goosefoot—*continued*
  Red   Chenopodium rubrum
  Stinking   vulvaria
  Upright   urbicum

Gorse   Ulex europaeus
  Dwarf   minor
  Western   gallii

Grape *see also* Oregon-g.

Grape-vine   Vitis vinifera

Grass *see* Introduction for
    treatment of grasses

Grass-of-Parnassus   Parnassia palustris

Grass-poly   Lythrum hyssopifolia

Greenweed, Dyer's   Genista tinctoria
  Hairy   pilosa

Gromwell, Common   Lithospermum officinale
  Field   arvense
  Purple   purpurocaeruleum

Ground-elder   Aegopodium podagraria

Ground-ivy   Glechoma hederacea

Ground-pine   Ajuga chamaepitys

Groundsel   Senecio vulgaris
  Heath   sylvaticus
  Sticky   viscosus

Guelder-rose   Viburnum opulus

Hair-grass, Alpine   Deschampsia alpina
  Bog   setacea
  Crested   Koeleria cristata
  Early   Aira praecox
  Grey   Corynephorus canescens
  Silver   Aira caryophyllea
  Somerset   Koeleria vallesiana
  Tufted   Deschampsia cespitosa
  Wavy   flexuosa

Hairy-brome	Bromus ramosus
Lesser	benekenii
Hampshire-purslane	Ludwigia palustris
Hard-grass	Parapholis strigosa
Curved	incurva
Harebell	Campanula rotundifolia
Hare's-ear, Shrubby	Bupleurum fruticosum
Sickle-leaved	falcatum
Slender	tenuissimum
Small	baldense
Hare's-tail	Lagurus ovatus
Hart's-tongue	Phyllitis scolopendrium
Hartwort	Tordylium maximum
Hawkbit, Autumn	Leontodon autumnalis
Lesser	taraxacoides
Rough	hispidus
Hawk's-beard, Beaked	Crepis vesicaria subsp.
	taraxacifolia
Bristly	setosa
Marsh	paludosa
Northern	mollis
Rough	biennis
Smooth	capillaris
Stinking	foetida
Hawkweed	Hieracium murorum*
Mouse-ear	pilosella
Hawthorn	Crataegus monogyna
Midland	laevigata (Poir.) DC.
Hazel	Corylus avellana

Heath *see also* Sea-h.

Heath, Blue	Phyllodoce caerulea
Cornish	Erica vagans

* There are numerous microspecies which, if correctly identified, should be so indicated.

Heath—*continued*
  Corsican   Erica terminalis
  Cross-leaved   tetralix
  Dorset   ciliaris
  Irish   erigena R. Ross
  Mackay's   mackaiana
  Prickly   Pernettya mucronata
  St. Dabeoc's   Daboecia cantabrica

Heather   Calluna vulgaris
  Bell   Erica cinerea

Heath-grass   Sieglingia decumbens

Hedge-parsley, Knotted   Torilis nodosa
  Spreading   arvensis
  Upright   japonica

Heliotrope, Winter   Petasites fragrans

Hellebore, Green   Helleborus viridis
  Stinking   foetidus

Helleborine, Broad-leaved   Epipactis helleborine
  Dark-red   atrorubens
  Dune   dunensis
  Green-flowered   phyllanthes
  Marsh   palustris
  Narrow-leaved   Cephalanthera longifolia
  Narrow-lipped   Epipactis leptochila
  Red   Cephalanthera rubra
  Violet   Epipactis purpurata
  White   Cephalanthera damasonium

Hemlock   Conium maculatum

Hemp-agrimony   Eupatorium cannabinum

Hemp-nettle, Common   Galeopsis tetrahit
  Downy   segetum
  Large-flowered   speciosa
  Red   angustifolia

Henbane   Hyoscyamus niger

Herb-Paris   Paris quadrifolia

Herb-Robert   Geranium robertianum

Hogweed   Heracleum sphondylium
  Giant   mantegazzianum

Holly *see also* Sea-h.

Holly	Ilex aquifolium
Holy-grass	Hierochloe odorata
Honesty	Lunaria annua
Honewort	Trinia glauca

Honeysuckle
  Fly
  Himalayan
  Perfoliate
	Lonicera periclymenum
	    xylosteum
	Leycesteria formosa
	Lonicera caprifolium

Hop	Humulus lupulus
Horehound, Black White	Ballota nigra Marrubium vulgare
Hornbeam	Carpinus betulus
Horned-poppy, Violet Yellow	Roemeria hybrida Glaucium flavum

Hornwort, Rigid
  Soft
	Ceratophyllum demersum
	    submersum

Horse-chestnut	Aesculus hippocastanum
Horse-radish	Armoracia rusticana

Horsetail, Field
  Great
  Marsh
  Rough
  Shady
  Variegated
  Water
  Wood
	Equisetum arvense
	    telmateia
	    palustre
	    hyemale
	    pratense
	    variegatum
	    fluviatile
	    sylvaticum

Hottentot-fig	Carpobrotus edulis

Hound's-tongue
  Green
	Cynoglossum officinale
	    germanicum

House-leek	Sempervivum tectorum
Hutchinsia	Hornungia petraea

Hyacinth, Grape	Muscari atlanticum
Hyssop	Hyssopus officinalis
Iceland-purslane	Koenigia islandica
Iris, Blue	Iris spuria
Purple	versicolor
Snake's-head	Hermodactylus tuberosus
Stinking	Iris foetidissima
Yellow	pseudacorus

Ivy *see also* Ground-i.

Ivy	Hedera helix
Jacob's-ladder	Polemonium caeruleum
Juneberry	Amelanchier confusa
Juniper	Juniperus communis

Kale *see* Sea-k.

Knapweed, Brown	Centaurea jacea
Common	nigra
Greater	scabiosa
Jersey	paniculata
Slender	nemoralis
Knawel, Annual	Scleranthus annuus
Perennial	perennis
Knotgrass	Polygonum aviculare
Ray's	raii
Sea	maritimum
Knotweed, Giant	Polygonum sachalinense
Himalayan	polystachyum
Japanese	cuspidatum
Lesser	campanulatum
Labrador-tea	Ledum groenlandicum
Laburnum	Laburnum anagyroides

Lady-fern Alpine	Athyrium filix-femina distentifolium Tausch ex Opiz
Lady's-mantle Alpine	Alchemilla vulgaris* alpina
Lady's-slipper	Cypripedium calceolus
Lady's-tresses, Autumn Creeping Irish Summer	Spiranthes spiralis Goodyera repens Spiranthes romanzoffiana aestivalis
Larch,European	Larix decidua
Larkspur	Delphinium ambiguum
Laurel *see also* Spurge-l.	
Laurel, Cherry Portugal	Prunus laurocerasus lusitanica
Laurustinus	Viburnum tinus
Lavender *see* Sea-l.	
Leek *see also* House-l.	
Leek, Babington's Few-flowered Round-headed Sand Three-cornered Wild	Allium babingtonii paradoxum sphaerocephalon scorodoprasum triquetrum ampeloprasum
Leopard's-bane Plantain-leaved	Doronicum pardalianches plantagineum
Lettuce, Great Least Prickly Wall	Lactuca virosa saligna serriola Mycelis muralis
Lilac	Syringa vulgaris

Lily *see also* Water-l.

* There are a number of microspecies which, if correctly identified, should be so indicated.

Lily, Kerry	Simethis planifolia
Martagon	Lilium martagon
May	Maianthemum bifolium
Pyrenean	Lilium pyrenaicum
Snowdon	Lloydia serotina
Lily-of-the-valley	Convallaria majalis
Lime	Tilia × vulgaris Hayne
Large-leaved	platyphyllos
Small-leaved	cordata
Liquorice, Wild	Astragalus glycyphyllos
Little-Robin	Geranium purpureum
Lobelia, Heath	Lobelia urens
Water	dortmanna
Londonpride	Saxifraga umbrosa
London-rocket	Sisymbrium irio
False	loeselii
Longleaf	Falcaria vulgaris
Loosestrife, Dotted	Lysimachia punctata
Fringed	ciliata
Lake	terrestris
Tufted	thyrsiflora
Yellow	vulgaris
Lords-and-Ladies	Arum maculatum
Italian	italicum
Lousewort	Pedicularis sylvatica
Marsh	palustris
Lovage, Scots	Ligusticum scoticum
Lucerne	Medicago sativa
Lungwort	Pulmonaria officinalis
Narrow-leaved	longifolia
Lupin, Nootka	Lupinus nootkatensis
Tree	arboreus
Lyme-grass	Elymus arenarius

Madder, Field	Sherardia arvensis
Wild	Rubia peregrina
Madwort	Asperugo procumbens
Male-fern	Dryopteris filix-mas
Scaly	pseudomas (Wollaston) Holub & Pouzar

Mallow *see also* Marsh-m.,
   Tree-m.

Mallow, Chinese	Malva verticillata
Common	sylvestris
Dwarf	neglecta
Least	parviflora
Musk	moschata
Small	pusilla
Maple, Field	Acer campestre
Norway	platanoides
Mare's-tail	Hippuris vulgaris

Marigold *see also* Bur-m.,
   Marsh-m.

Marigold, Corn	Chrysanthemum segetum
Field	Calendula arvensis
Pot	officinalis
Marjoram	Origanum vulgare
Marram	Ammophila arenaria
Marsh-bedstraw, Common	Galium palustre
Slender	debile
Marsh-mallow	Althaea officinalis
Rough	hirsuta
Marsh-marigold	Caltha palustris
Marsh-orchid, Early	Dactylorhiza incarnata (L.) Soó
Irish	kerryensis (Wilmott) Hunt & Summerh.
Narrow-leaved	traunsteineri(Sauter) Soó
Northern	purpurella (T. & T. A. Stephenson) Soó
Southern	praetermissa (Druce) Soó

Marshwort, Creeping	Apium repens
Lesser	inundatum
Masterwort	Peucedanum ostruthium
Mat-grass	Nardus stricta
Mayweed, Scented	Matricaria recutita
Scentless	Tripleurospermum
	maritimum subsp.
	inodorum
Meadow-grass, Alpine	Poa alpina
Annual	annua
Broad-leaved	chaixii
Bulbous	bulbosa
Early	infirma
Flattened	compressa
Glaucous	glauca
Narrow-leaved	angustifolia
Rough	trivialis
Smooth	pratensis
Spreading	subcaerulea
Swamp	palustris
Wavy	flexuosa
Wood	nemoralis
Meadow-rue, Alpine	Thalictrum alpinum
Common	flavum
Lesser	minus
Meadowsweet	Filipendula ulmaria
Medick, Black	Medicago lupulina
Bur	minima
Sickle	falcata
Spotted	arabica
Toothed	polymorpha
Medlar	Mespilus germanica
Melick, Mountain	Melica nutans
Wood	uniflora
Melilot, Ribbed	Melilotus officinalis
Small	indica
Tall	altissima
White	alba

Mercury, Annual	Mercurialis annua
Dog's	perennis
Mezereon	Daphne mezereum
Michaelmas-daisy	Aster novi-belgii*
Mignonette, White	Reseda alba
Wild	lutea
Milfoil *see* Water-m.	
Milk-parsley	Peucedanum palustre
Cambridge	Selinum carvifolia
Milk-vetch, Alpine	Astragalus alpinus
Purple	danicus
Milkwort *see also* Sea-m.	
Milkwort, Chalk	Polygala calcarea
Common	vulgaris
Dwarf	amara
Heath	serpyllifolia
Millet, Early	Milium scabrum
Wood	effusum
Mind-your-own-business	Soleirolia soleirolii (Req.)
	Dandy
Mint, Corn	Mentha arvensis
Corsican	requienii
Horse	longifolia
Round-leaved	rotundifolia
Spear	spicata
Water	aquatica
Mistletoe	Viscum album
Moneywort, Cornish	Sibthorpia europaea
Monkeyflower	Mimulus guttatus
Monk's-hood	Aconitum napellus

* This is probably the most common of a number of closely allied species. If a correct identification has been made this should be so indicated.

Monk's-rhubarb	Rumex alpinus
Montbretia	Crocosmia × crocosmiflora
Moonwort	Botrychium lunaria
Moor-grass, Blue	Sesleria caerulea
Purple	Molinia caerulea
Moschatel	Adoxa moschatellina
Motherwort	Leonurus cardiaca
Mouse-ear, Alpine	Cerastium alpinum
Arctic	arcticum
Common	holosteoides
Dwarf	pumilum
Field	arvense
Grey	brachypetalum
Little	semidecandrum
Sea	diffusum Pers.
Shetland	nigrescens
Starwort	cerastoides
Sticky	glomeratum
Mousetail	Myosurus minimus
Mudwort	Limosella aquatica
Welsh	australis R.Br.
Mugwort	Artemisia vulgaris
Chinese	verlotorum
Hoary	stellerana
Norwegian	norvegica
Mullein, Dark	Verbascum nigrum
Great	thapsus
Hoary	pulverulentum
Moth	blattaria
Orange	phlomoides
Twiggy	virgatum
White	lychnitis
Musk	Mimulus moschatus
Mustard, Black	Brassica nigra
Garlic	Alliaria petiolata
Hare's-ear	Conringia orientalis
Hedge	Sisymbrium officinale

Mustard—*continued*	
Hoary	Hirschfeldia incana
Tower	Turritis glabra
Treacle	Erysimum cheiranthoides
White	Sinapis alba
Myrtle, Bog	Myrica gale
Naiad, Holly-leaved	Najas marina
Slender	flexilis
Navelwort	Umbilicus rupestris
Nettle *see also* Dead-n., Hemp-n.	
Nettle, Common	Urtica dioica
Roman	pilulifera
Small	urens
Nightshade *see also* Enchanter's-n.	
Nightshade, Black	Solanum nigrum
Deadly	Atropa belladonna
Green	Solanum sarrachoides
Nipplewort	Lapsana communis
Nit-grass	Gastridium ventricosum
Oak, Evergreen	Quercus ilex
Pedunculate	robur
Sessile	petraea
Turkey	cerris
Oat, *see also* Wild-o.	
Oat, Bristle	Avena strigosa
Oat-grass, Downy	Helictotrichon pubescens
False	Arrhenatherum elatius
Meadow	Helictotrichon pratense
Yellow	Trisetum flavescens
Onion, Wild	Allium vineale

Orache, Babington's	Atriplex glabriuscula
Common	patula
Frosted	laciniata
Garden	hortensis
Grass-leaved	littoralis
Shrubby	halimus
Spear-leaved	hastata

Orchid *see also* Butterfly-o.,
　　Marsh-o., Spider-o.

Orchid, Bee	Ophrys apifera
Bird's-nest	Neottia nidus-avis
Bog	Hammarbya paludosa
Burnt	Orchis ustulata
Coralroot	Corallorhiza trifida
Dense-flowered	Neotinea intacta
Early-purple	Orchis mascula
Fen	Liparis loeselii
Fly	Ophrys insectifera
Fragrant	Gymnadenia conopsea
Frog	Coeloglossum viride
Ghost	Epipogium aphyllum
Green-winged	Orchis morio
Lady	purpurea
Lizard	Himantoglossum hircinum
Loose-flowered	Orchis laxiflora
Man	Aceras anthropophorum
Military	Orchis militaris
Monkey	simia
Musk	Herminium monorchis
Pyramidal	Anacamptis pyramidalis
Small-white	Pseudorchis albida (L.)
	A. & D. Löve

Oregon-grape	Mahonia aquifolium
Orpine	Sedum telephium
Osier	Salix viminalis
Oxlip	Primula elatior
Oxtongue, Bristly	Picris echioides
Hawkweed	hieracioides
Oxytropis, Purple	Oxytropis halleri
Yellow	campestris

Oysterplant	Mertensia maritima
Pampas-grass	Cortaderia selloana
Pansy, Dwarf	Viola kitaibeliana
Field	arvensis
Mountain	lutea
Wild	tricolor
Parsley *see also* Bur-p., Hedge-p., Milk-p.	
Parsley, Corn	Petroselinum segetum
Cow	Anthriscus sylvestris
Fool's	Aethusa cynapium
Garden	Petroselinum crispum
Stone	Sison amomum
Parsley-piert	Aphanes arvensis
Slender	microcarpa
Parsnip *see also* Water-p.	
Parsnip, Wild	Pastinaca sativa
Pasqueflower	Pulsatilla vulgaris
Pea *see also* Everlasting-p.	
Pea, Black	Lathyrus niger
Marsh	palustris
Sea	japonicus
Tuberous	tuberosus
Pear, Wild	Pyrus communis
Pearlwort, Alpine	Sagina saginoides
Annual	apetala
Heath	subulata
Knotted	nodosa
Procumbent	procumbens
Scottish	normaniana
Sea	maritima
Snow	intermedia
Pellitory-of-the-wall	Parietaria judaica L.
Penny-cress, Alpine	Thlaspi alpestre
Field	arvense

Penny-cress—*continued*
  Garlic   Thlaspi alliaceum
  Perfoliate   perfoliatum

Pennyroyal   Mentha pulegium

Pennywort, Marsh   Hydrocotyle vulgaris

Peony   Paeonia mascula

Pepper *see* Water-p.

Pepper-saxifrage   Silaum silaus

Pepperwort, Field   Lepidium campestre
  Least   neglectum
  Narrow-leaved   ruderale
  Smith's   heterophyllum
  Tall   graminifolium

Periwinkle, Greater   Vinca major
  Lesser   minor

Persicaria, Pale   Polygonum lapathifolium

Pheasant's-eye   Adonis annua

Pick-a-back-plant   Tolmiea menziesii

Pignut   Conopodium majus
  Great   Bunium bulbocastanum

Pillwort   Pilularia globulifera

Pimpernel, Blue   Anagallis foemina
  Bog   tenella
  Scarlet   arvensis
  Yellow   Lysimachia nemorum

Pine *see also* Ground-p.

Pine, Maritime   Pinus pinaster
  Scots   sylvestris

Pineappleweed   Matricaria matricarioides

Pink   Dianthus plumarius
  Cheddar   gratianopolitanus
  Childling   Petrorhagia nanteuilii
                    (Burnat) Ball &
                    Heywood

Pink—*continued*
   Clove   Dianthus caryophyllus
   Deptford   armeria
   Jersey   gallicus
   Maiden   deltoides

Pipewort   Eriocaulon aquaticum (Hill)
                        Druce

Pirri-pirri-bur   Acaena anserinifolia

Pitcherplant   Sarracenia purpurea

Plane, London   Platanus × hybrida

Plantain *see also* Water-p.

Plantain, Buck's-horn Plantago coronopus
   Greater   major
   Hoary   media
   Ribwort   lanceolata
   Sea   maritima

Ploughman's-spikenard Inula conyza

Plum, Cherry   Prunus cerasifera
   Wild   domestica

Polypody   Polypodium vulgare

Pond-sedge, Greater   Carex riparia
   Lesser   acutiformis

Pondweed, American   Potamogeton epihydrus
   Blunt-leaved   obtusifolius
   Bog   polygonifolius
   Broad-leaved   natans
   Curled   crispus
   Fen   coloratus
   Fennel   pectinatus
   Flat-stalked   friesii
   Grass-wrack   compressus
   Hairlike   trichoides
   Horned   Zannichellia palustris
   Lesser   Potamogeton pusillus
   Loddon   nodosus
   Long-stalked   praelongus
   Opposite-leaved   Groenlandia densa
   Perfoliate   Potamogeton perfoliatus

Pondweed—*continued*
  Red   Potamogeton alpinus
  Sharp-leaved   acutifolius
  Shetland   rutilus
  Shining   lucens
  Slender-leaved   filiformis
  Small   berchtoldii
  Various-leaved   gramineus

Poplar, Balsam   Populus gileadensis
  Black   nigra
  Grey   canescens
  Italian   × canadensis
  White   alba

Poppy *see also* Horned-p.

Poppy, Californian   Eschscholzia californica
  Common   Papaver rhoeas
  Long-headed   dubium
  Opium   somniferum
  Prickly   argemone
  Rough   hybridum
  Welsh   Meconopsis cambrica
  Yellow-juiced   Papaver lecoqii

Primrose *see also* Evening-p.

Primrose   Primula vulgaris
  Bird's-eye   farinosa
  Scottish   scotica

Primrose-peerless   Narcissus × medioluteus Mill.

Privet, Garden   Ligustrum ovalifolium
  Wild   vulgare

Purple-loosestrife   Lythrum salicaria

Purslane *see also*
      Hampshire-p.,
      Iceland-p., Sea-p.,
      Water-p.

Purslane, Pink   Montia sibirica

Quaking-grass   Briza media
  Great   maxima
  Lesser   minor

Quillwort	Isoetes lacustris
Land	histrix
Spring	echinospora

Radish *see also* Horse-r.

Radish, Garden	Raphanus sativus
Sea	maritimus
Wild	raphanistrum

Ragged-Robin — Lychnis flos-cuculi

Ragweed — Ambrosia artemisiifolia

Ragwort, Broad-leaved	Senecio fluviatilis
Common	jacobaea
Fen	paludosus
Hoary	erucifolius
Magellan	smithii
Marsh	aquaticus
Oxford	squalidus
Silver	cineraria

Ramping-fumitory, Common	Fumaria muralis subsp. boraei
Purple	purpurea
Tall	bastardii
White	capreolata

Rampion, Round-headed	Phyteuma tenerum
Spiked	spicatum

Ramsons — Allium ursinum

Rannoch-rush — Scheuchzeria palustris

Rape — Brassica napus

Raspberry — Rubus idaeus

Rattle, Yellow — Rhinanthus minor

Redshank — Polygonum persicaria

Reed *see also* Bur-r., Small-r.

Reed, Common — Phragmites australis (Cav.). Trin. ex Steud.

Restharrow, Common	Ononis repens
Small	reclinata
Spiny	spinosa
Rhododendron	Rhododendron ponticum

Rhubarb *see* Monk's-r.

Rock-cress, Alpine	Arabis alpina
Bristol	scabra All.
Fringed	brownii
Hairy	hirsuta
Northern	Cardaminopsis petraea

Rocket *see also* London-r.

Rocket, Eastern	Sisymbrium orientale
Hairy	Erucastrum gallicum
Sea	Cakile maritima
Tall	Sisymbrium altissimum
White	Diplotaxis erucoides
Rock-rose, Common	Helianthemum chamaecistus
Hoary	canum
Spotted	Tuberaria guttata
White	Helianthemum apenninum

Rose *see also* Guelder-r.,
    Rock-r.

Rose, Burnet	Rosa pimpinellifolia
Dog	canina*
Downy	villosa†
Field	arvensis
Japanese	rugosa
Rosemary, Bog	Andromeda polifolia
Rose-of-Sharon	Hypericum calycinum
Roseroot	Sedum rosea

---

* The English name may be applied also to *R.dumalis* and *R.obtusifolia*. If a correct identification has been made this should be indicated.
† The English name may be applied also to *R.tomentosa* and *R.sherardii*. If a correct identification has been made this should be indicated.

Rowan	Sorbus aucuparia
Rue *see* Goat's-r, Meadow-r., Wall-r.	
Rupturewort, Fringed	Herniaria ciliolata
Smooth	glabra
Rush *see also* Bog-r., Club-r., Flowering-r., Rannoch-r., Spike-r., Wood-r.	
Rush, Alpine	Juncus alpinoarticulatus
Baltic	balticus
Blunt-flowered	subnodulosus
Bulbous	bulbosus
Chestnut	castaneus
Compact	subuliflorus Drejer
Dwarf	capitatus
Hard	inflexus
Heath	squarrosus
Jointed	articulatus
Marshall's	nodulosus
Pigmy	mutabilis
Round-fruited	compressus
Saltmarsh	gerardii
Sea	maritimus
Sharp	acutus
Sharp-flowered	acutiflorus
Slender	tenuis
Soft	effusus
Thread	filiformis
Three-flowered	triglumis
Three-leaved	trifidus
Toad	bufonius
Two-flowered	biglumis
Russian-vine	Polygonum aubertii L. Henry
Rustyback	Ceterach officinarum
Rye-grass, Italian	Lolium multiflorum
Perennial	perenne
Saffron, Meadow	Colchicum autumnale
Sage, Wood	Teucrium scorodonia

Sainfoin	Onobrychis viciifolia
St. John's-wort, Flax-leaved	Hypericum linarifolium
Hairy	hirsutum
Imperforate	maculatum
Irish	canadense
Marsh	elodes
Pale	montanum
Perforate	perforatum
Slender	pulchrum
Square-stalked	tetrapterum
Trailing	humifusum
Wavy	undulatum
St. Patrick's-cabbage	Saxifraga spathularis
Salsify	Tragopogon porrifolius
Saltmarsh-grass, Borrer's	Puccinellia fasciculata
Common	maritima
Greater	pseudodistans
Northern	capillaris
Reflexed	distans
Stiff	rupestris
Saltwort, Prickly	Salsola kali
Spineless	pestifer
Samphire, Golden	Inula crithmoides
Rock	Crithmum maritimum
Sand-grass, Early	Mibora minima
Sandwort, Arctic	Arenaria norvegica subsp. norvegica
English	norvegica subsp. anglica Halliday
Fine-leaved	Minuartia hybrida
Fringed	Arenaria ciliata subsp. hibernica
Mossy	balearica
Mountain	Minuartia rubella
Sea	Honkenya peploides
Slender	Arenaria leptoclados
Spring	Minuartia verna
Teesdale	stricta
Three-nerved	Moehringia trinervia
Thyme-leaved	Arenaria serpyllifolia
Sanicle	Sanicula europaea

Savory, Winter	Satureja montana
Saw-wort	Serratula tinctoria
Alpine	Saussurea alpina

Saxifrage *see also* Burnet-s.,
    Golden-s., Pepper-s.

Saxifrage, Alpine	Saxifraga nivalis
Drooping	cernua
Highland	rivularis
Irish	rosacea
Kidney	hirsuta
Marsh	hirculus
Meadow	granulata
Mossy	hypnoides
Purple	oppositifolia
Rue-leaved	tridactylites
Starry	stellaris
Tufted	cespitosa
Yellow	aizoides
Scabious, Devil's-bit	Succisa pratensis
Field	Knautia arvensis
Small	Scabiosa columbaria
Scurvygrass, Alpine	Cochlearia alpina
Common	officinalis
Danish	danica
English	anglica
Scottish	scotica
Sea-blite, Annual	Suaeda maritima
Shrubby	vera J. F. Gmel.
Sea-buckthorn	Hippophae rhamnoides
Sea-heath	Frankenia laevis
Sea-holly	Eryngium maritimum
Sea-kale	Crambe maritima
Sea-lavender, Alderney	Limonium auriculae- ursifolium
Common	vulgare
Lax-flowered	humile
Matted	bellidifolium
Rock	binervosum

Sea-milkwort	Glaux maritima
Sea-purslane	Halimione portulacoides
Sea-spurrey, Greater	Spergularia media
Lesser	marina
Rock	rupicola

Sedge *see also* Alpine-s.,
      Beak-s., Bladder-s.,
      Bog-s., Fen-s., Flat-s.,
      Fox-s., Pond-s.,
      Tufted-s., Tussock-s.,
      Wood-s., Yellow-s.

Sedge, Bird's-foot	Carex ornithopoda
Bottle	rostrata
Bristle	microglochin
Brown	disticha
Carnation	panicea
Club	buxbaumii
Common	nigra
Curved	maritima
Cyperus	pseudocyperus
Dioecious	dioica
Distant	distans
Divided	divisa
Dotted	punctata
Downy-fruited	filiformis
Dwarf	humilis
Elongated	elongata
Estuarine	recta
False	Kobresia simpliciuscula
Few-flowered	Carex pauciflora
Fingered	digitata
Flea	pulicaris
Glaucous	flacca
Green-ribbed	binervis
Grey	divulsa
Hair	capillaris
Hairy	hirta
Hare's-foot	lachenalii
Long-bracted	extensa
Oval	ovalis
Pale	pallescens
Pendulous	pendula
Pill	pilulifera
Prickly	muricata
Remote	remota

Sedge—*continued*
Rock	Carex rupestris
Russet	saxatilis
Sand	arenaria
Sheathed	vaginata
Slender	lasiocarpa
Smooth-stalked	laevigata
Soft-leaved	montana
Spiked	spicata
Star	echinata
Stiff	bigelowii
String	chordorrhiza
Tawny	hostiana
Water	aquatilis
White	curta

Selfheal	Prunella vulgaris
Cut-leaved	laciniata

Service-tree	Sorbus domestica
Wild	torminalis

Shallon — Gaultheria shallon

Sheep's-bit — Jasione montana

Sheep's-fescue	Festuca ovina
Fine-leaved	tenuifolia

Shepherd's-needle — Scandix pecten-veneris

Shepherd's-purse — Capsella bursa-pastoris

Shield-fern, Hard	Polystichum aculeatum
Soft	setiferum

Shoreweed — Littorella uniflora

Sibbaldia — Sibbaldia procumbens

Silky-bent, Dense	Apera interrupta
Loose	spica-venti

Silverweed — Potentilla anserina

Skullcap	Scutellaria galericulata
Lesser	minor

Small-reed, Narrow — Calamagrostis stricta

Small-reed—*continued*

Purple	Calamagrostis canescens
Scottish	scotica
Wood	epigejos

Snapdragon	Antirrhinum majus
Lesser	Misopates orontium

Sneezewort	Achillea ptarmica

Snowberry	Symphoricarpos rivularis

Snowdrop	Galanthus nivalis

Snowflake, Spring	Leucojum vernum
Summer	aestivum

Snow-in-summer	Cerastium tomentosum

Soapwort	Saponaria officinalis

Soft-brome	Bromus mollis
Least	ferronii
Lesser	thominii
Slender	lepidus

Soft-grass, Creeping	Holcus mollis

Soldier *see also* Water-s.

Soldier, Gallant	Galinsoga parviflora
Shaggy	ciliata

Solomon's-seal	Polygonatum multiflorum
Angular	odoratum
Whorled	verticillatum

Sorrel *see also* Wood-s.

Sorrel, Common	Rumex acetosa
French	scutatus
Mountain	Oxyria digyna
Sheep's	Rumex acetosella

Sow-thistle, Alpine	Cicerbita alpina
Blue	macrophylla
Marsh	Sonchus palustris
Perennial	arvensis
Prickly	asper
Smooth	oleraceus

Spearwort, Adder's-tongue	Ranunculus ophioglossifolius
Creeping	reptans
Greater	lingua
Lesser	flammula

Speedwell *see also* Field-s.,
    Water-s.

Speedwell, Alpine	Veronica alpina
American	peregrina
Breckland	praecox
Fingered	triphyllos
Germander	chamaedrys
Heath	officinalis
Ivy-leaved	hederifolia
Marsh	scutellata
Rock	fruticans
Slender	filiformis
Spiked	spicata
Spring	verna
Thyme-leaved	serpyllifolia
Wall	arvensis
Wood	montana

Spider-orchid, Early	Ophrys sphegodes
Late	fuciflora

Spignel	Meum athamanticum

Spike-rush, Common	Eleocharis palustris
Dwarf	parvula
Few-flowered	quinqueflora
Many-stalked	multicaulis
Needle	acicularis
Northern	austriaca
Slender	uniglumis

Spindle	Euonymus europaeus

Spleenwort, Black	Asplenium adiantum-nigrum
Forked	septentrionale
Green	viride
Lanceolate	billotii F. W. Schultz
Maidenhair	trichomanes
Sea	marinum

Spotted-orchid, Common	Dactylorhiza fuchsii (Druce) Soó
Heath	maculata (L.) Soó

Springbeauty	Montia perfoliata

Spring-sedge
  Rare
	Carex caryophyllea
	  ericetorum

Spruce, Norway
  Sitka
	Picea abies
	  sitchensis

Spurge, Broad-leaved
  Caper
  Coral
  Cypress
  Dwarf
  Hairy
	Euphorbia platyphyllos
	  lathyrus
	  corallioides
	  cyparissias
	  exigua
	  villosa Waldst. & Kit. ex
	    Willd.

Irish
  Leafy
  Petty
  Portland
  Purple
  Sea
  Sun
  Sweet
  Twiggy
  Upright
  Wood
	hyberna
	  esula
	  peplus
	  portlandica
	  peplis
	  paralias
	  helioscopia
	  dulcis
	  uralensis
	  serrulata Thuill.
	  amygdaloides

Spurge-laurel	Daphne laureola
Spurrey *see also* Sea-s.	
Spurrey, Corn Sand	Spergula arvensis Spergularia rubra

Squill, Autumn
  Spring
	Scilla autumnalis
	  verna

Squinancywort	Asperula cynanchica
Starfruit	Damasonium alisma

Star-of-Bethlehem
  Drooping
  Spiked
  Yellow
	Ornithogalum umbellatum
	  nutans
	  pyrenaicum
	Gagea lutea

Star-thistle, Red
  Rough
  Yellow
	Centaurea calcitrapa
	  aspera
	  solstitialis

Starwort *see* Water-s.	

Stitchwort, Bog	Stellaria alsine
Greater	holostea
Lesser	graminea
Marsh	palustris
Wood	nemorum
Stock, Hoary	Matthiola incana
Sea	sinuata
Stonecrop, Biting	Sedum acre
English	anglicum
Hairy	villosum
Mossy	Crassula tillaea
Reflexed	Sedum reflexum
Rock	forsteranum
Tasteless	sexangulare
Thick-leaved	dasyphyllum
White	album
Stork's-bill, Common	Erodium cicutarium
Musk	moschatum
Sea	maritimum
Sticky	glutinosum
Strapwort	Corrigiola litoralis
Strawberry, Barren	Potentilla sterilis
Garden	Fragaria ananassa
Wild	vesca
Strawberry-blite	Chenopodium capitatum
Strawberry-tree	Arbutus unedo
Succory, Lamb's	Arnoseris minima
Sundew, Great	Drosera anglica
Oblong-leaved	intermedia
Round-leaved	rotundifolia
Sweet-flag	Acorus calamus
Sweet-grass, Floating	Glyceria fluitans
Plicate	plicata
Reed	maxima
Small	declinata
Sweet-William	Dianthus barbatus

Swine-cress

Swine-cress	Coronopus squamatus
Lesser	didymus
Sycamore	Acer pseudoplatanus
Tamarisk	Tamarix anglica*
Tansy	Tanacetum vulgare L.
Tare, Hairy	Vicia hirsuta
Slender	tenuissima
Smooth	tetrasperma
Tasselweed, Beaked	Ruppia maritima
Spiral	cirrhosa (Petagna) Grande

Tea *see* Labrador-t.

Teaplant, China	Lycium chinense
Duke of Argyll's	barbarum L.
Teasel	Dipsacus fullonum
Small	pilosus

Thistle *see also* Sow-t., Star-t.

Thistle, Cabbage	Cirsium oleraceum
Carline	Carlina vulgaris
Cotton	Onopordon acanthium
Creeping	Cirsium arvense
Dwarf	acaule Scop.
Marsh	palustre
Meadow	dissectum
Melancholy	heterophyllum
Milk	Silybum marianum
Musk	Carduus nutans
Plymouth	pycnocephalus
Slender	tenuiflorus
Spear	Cirsium vulgare
Tuberous	tuberosum
Welted	Carduus acanthoides
Woolly	Cirsium eriophorum
Thorn-apple	Datura stramonium

* The English name may also be applied to the closely allied species *T.gallica.*

Thorow-wax	Bupleurum rotundifolium
False	lancifolium
Thrift	Armeria maritima
Jersey	arenaria
Thyme, Basil	Acinos arvensis
Breckland	Thymus serpyllum
Large	pulegioides
Wild	drucei
Timothy	Phleum pratense

Toadflax *see also* Bastard-t.

Toadflax, Common	Linaria vulgaris
Ivy-leaved	Cymbalaria muralis
Jersey	Linaria pelisseriana
Pale	repens
Prostrate	supina
Purple	purpurea
Sand	arenaria
Small	Chaenorhinum minus
Toothwort	Lathraea squamaria
Purple	clandestina
Tor-grass	Brachypodium pinnatum
Tormentil	Potentilla erecta
Trailing	anglica
Traveller's-joy	Clematis vitalba
Tree-mallow	Lavatera arborea
Small	cretica

Trefoil *see also* Bird's-foot-t.

Trefoil, Hop	Trifolium campestre
Lesser	dubium
Slender	micranthum
Tufted-sedge	Carex elata
Slender	acuta
Tulip, Wild	Tulipa sylvestris
Turnip, Wild	Brassica rapa

Tussock-sedge, Fibrous	Carex appropinquata
Greater	paniculata
Lesser	diandra
Tutsan	Hypericum androsaemum
Stinking	hircinum
Tall	inodorum Mill.
Twayblade, Common	Listera ovata
Lesser	cordata
Twinflower	Linnaea borealis
Valerian, Common	Valeriana officinalis
Marsh	dioica
Pyrenean	pyrenaica
Red	Centranthus ruber
Venus's-looking-glass	Legousia hybrida
Vernal-grass, Annual	Anthoxanthum puelii
Sweet	odoratum
Vervain	Verbena officinalis

Vetch *see also* Bitter-v.,
 Milk-v., Yellow-v.

Vetch, Bithynian	Vicia bithynica
Bitter*	Lathyrus montanus
Bush	Vicia sepium
Common	sativa
Crown	Coronilla varia
Fine-leaved	Vicia tenuifolia
Fodder	villosa†
Horseshoe	Hippocrepis comosa
Kidney	Anthyllis vulneraria
Narrow-leaved	Vicia angustifolia
Spring	lathyroides
Tufted	cracca
Wood	sylvatica
Vetchling, Grass	Lathyrus nissolia
Hairy	hirsutus

* *see also* Wood Bitter-v.
† The English name may also be applied to the closely allied species *V.dasycarpa*.

Vetchling—*continued*
  Meadow   Lathyrus pratensis
  Yellow   aphaca

Vine *see* Grape-v., Russian-v.

Violet *see also* Dame's-v.,
    Dog-v., Water-v.

Violet, Fen   Viola persicifolia Schreb.
  Hairy   hirta
  Marsh   palustris
  Sweet   odorata
  Teesdale   rupestris

Viper's-bugloss   Echium vulgare
  Purple   lycopsis

Viper's-grass   Scorzonera humilis

Wallflower   Cheiranthus cheiri

Wall-rocket, Annual   Diplotaxis muralis
  Perennial   tenuifolia

Wall-rue   Asplenium ruta-muraria

Walnut   Juglans regia

Water-cress   Rorippa nasturtium-
                                aquaticum
  Fool's   Apium nodiflorum

Water-crowfoot, Brackish   Ranunculus baudotii
  Common   aquatilis
  Fan-leaved   circinatus
  River   fluitans
  Thread-leaved   trichophyllus

Water-dropwort, Corky-   Oenanthe pimpinelloides
    fruited
  Fine-leaved   aquatica
  Hemlock   crocata
  Narrow-leaved   silaifolia
  Parsley   lachenalii
  River   fluviatilis
  Tubular   fistulosa

Water-lily, Fringed	Nymphoides peltata
Least	Nuphar pumila
White	Nymphaea alba
Yellow	Nuphar lutea
Water-milfoil, Alternate	Myriophyllum alterniflorum
Spiked	spicatum
Whorled	verticillatum
Water-parsnip, Greater	Sium latifolium
Lesser	Berula erecta
Water-pepper	Polygonum hydropiper
Small	minus
Tasteless	mite
Water-plantain	Alisma plantago-aquatica
Floating	Luronium natans
Lesser	Baldellia ranunculoides
Narrow-leaved	Alisma lanceolatum
Ribbon-leaved	gramineum
Water-purslane	Peplis portula
Water-soldier	Stratiotes aloides
Water-speedwell, Blue	Veronica anagallis-aquatica
Pink	catenata
Water-starwort, Autumnal	Callitriche hermaphroditica
Blunt-fruited	obtusangula
Common	stagnalis
Intermediate	intermedia
Short-leaved	truncata
Various-leaved	platycarpa
Water-violet	Hottonia palustris
Waterweed, Canadian	Elodea canadensis
Waterwort, Eight-stamened	Elatine hydropiper
Six-stamened	hexandra
Wayfaring-tree	Viburnum lantana
Weld	Reseda luteola
Whin, Petty	Genista anglica
Whitebeam, Broad-leaved	Sorbus latifolia* (*see* p. 119*)

Whitebeam—*continued*
  Common   Sorbus aria*
  Swedish   intermedia*

Whitlowgrass, Common   Erophila verna
  Hoary   Draba incana
  Rock   norvegica
  Round-podded   Erophila spathulata
  Wall   Draba muralis
  Yellow   aizoides

Whorl-grass   Catabrosa aquatica

Wild-oat   Avena fatua
  Winter   ludoviciana

Willow, Almond   Salix triandra
  Bay   pentandra
  Crack   fragilis
  Creeping   repens
  Dark-leaved   nigricans
  Downy   lapponum
  Dwarf   herbacea
  Eared   aurita
  Goat   caprea
  Grey   cinerea
  Mountain   arbuscula
  Net-leaved   reticulata
  Purple   purpurea
  Tea-leaved   phylicifolia
  White   alba
  Whortle-leaved   myrsinites
  Woolly   lanata

Willowherb, Alpine   Epilobium anagallidifolium
  American   adenocaulon
  Broad-leaved   montanum
  Chickweed   alsinifolium
  Great   hirsutum
  Hoary   parviflorum
  Marsh   palustre
  New Zealand   nerterioides
  Pale   roseum
  Rosebay   angustifolium L.
  Short-fruited   obscurum

* These Whitebeams comprise some closely allied species, most of which require expert determination. If this has been made it should be so indicated.

Willowherb—*continued*
Spear-leaved	Epilobium lanceolatum
Square-stalked	tetragonum L.

Winter-cress	Barbarea vulgaris
American	verna
Medium-flowered	intermedia
Small-flowered	stricta

Wintergreen, Chickweed	Trientalis europaea
Common	Pyrola minor
Intermediate	media
One-flowered	Moneses uniflora
Round-leaved	Pyrola rotundifolia
Serrated	Orthilia secunda

Woad	Isatis tinctoria

Woodruff	Galium odoratum
Pink	Asperula taurina

Wood-rush, Curved	Luzula arcuata
Fen	pallescens
Field	campestris
Great	sylvatica
Hairy	pilosa
Heath	multiflora
Southern	forsteri
Spiked	spicata
White	luzuloides

Wood-sedge	Carex sylvatica
Starved	depauperata
Thin-spiked	strigosa

Woodsia, Alpine	Woodsia alpina
Oblong	ilvensis

Wood-sorrel	Oxalis acetosella

Wormwood	Artemisia absinthium
Field	campestris
Sea	maritima

Woundwort, Downy	Stachys germanica
Field	arvensis
Hedge	sylvatica
Limestone	alpina
Marsh	palustris

Yarrow	Achillea millefolium
Yellow-cress, Austrian	Rorippa austriaca
Creeping	sylvestris
Great	amphibia
Marsh	islandica
Yellow-eyed-grass	Sisyrinchium californicum
Yellow-sedge, Common	Carex demissa
Large	flava
Long-stalked	lepidocarpa
Small-fruited	serotina
Yellow-vetch	Vicia lutea
Hairy	hybrida
Yellow-wort	Blackstonia perfoliata
Yew	Taxus baccata
Yorkshire-fog	Holcus lanatus